IEEE Computer Society
Real World Software
Engineering Problems

IEEE
Φ computer
society
60ᴛʜ anniversary

Press Operating Committee

IEEE Computer Society Publications
The world-renowned IEEE Computer Society publishes, promotes, and distributes a wide variety of authoritative computer science and engineering texts. These books are available from most retail outlets. Visit the CS Store at *http://computer.org/cspress* for a list of products.

IEEE Computer Society / Wiley Partnership
The IEEE Computer Society and Wiley partnership allows the CS Press authored book program to produce a number of exciting new titles in areas of computer science and engineering with a special focus on software engineering. IEEE Computer Society members continue to receive a 15% discount on these titles when purchased through Wiley or at wiley.com/ieeecs.

To submit questions about the program or send proposals please e-mail dplummer@computer.org or write to Books, IEEE Computer Society, 100662 Los Vaqueros Circle, Los Alamitos, CA 90720-1314. Telephone +1-714-821-8380.
Additional information regarding the Computer Society authored book program can also be accessed from our web site at *http://computer.org/cspress*.

IEEE Computer Society
Real World Software
Engineering Problems

A Self-Study Guide for Today's Software Professional

J. Fernando Naveda
Stephen B. Seidman

IEEE
computer
society
60TH anniversary

WILEY-
INTERSCIENCE

A JOHN WILEY & SONS, INC., PUBLICATION

Library of Congress Cataloging-in-Publication is available.

ISBN-13 978-0-471-71051-6
ISBN-10 0-471-71051-2

10 9 8 7 6 5 4 3

Preface

This software engineering problem book is the culmination of a team effort that has spanned more than three years. It originated as a suggestion made by Leonard Tripp, 1999 President of the IEEE Computer Society, at several meetings that were part of the Society's project to develop a certification examination for software engineering professionals.

In 2002, J. Fernando Naveda organized a group of volunteers to serve as leaders of teams to gather items for the book. Each leader recruited item writers, as follows: Mark Ardis (Mats Heimdahl, William F. Opdyke, Frank Young), Heidi J. C. Ellis (Vassilka Kirova, Patricia Pia), Susan K. Land (Darsi D. Ewing, Kathy Gaubon), Ana Maria Moreno (Oscar Dieste, Xavier Ferre, Natalia Juristo, Sira Vegas), and Matt Peloquin (Jenny Stuart, Steve Tockey). Led by J. Fernando Naveda, Stephanie Ludi and Judy Englert contributed a few extra items. Altogether, these teams produced 132 items, which were reviewed at a workshop held at the New Jersey Institute of Technology in the summer of 2002. The workshop participants were organized into three teams. Susan K. Land led a team consisting of Darsi D. Ewing, Robert Friedman, William F. Opdyke, and Thomas Rando. J. Fernando Naveda led a team consisting of Heidi J. C. Ellis, Mats Heimdahl, Ana Maria Moreno, and Frank Young. Matt Peloquin led a team consisting of Kathy Gaubon, Vassilka Kirova, Patricia Pia, and Jenny Stuart. The teams examined the items for quality and relevance, changed some of them, and wrote new items. By November 2002, 162 items had been produced.

Stephen Seidman then led an effort to further examine and refine this set of sample questions. He identified a group of CSDP certificate holders who were willing to evaluate these items. The members of this group of volunteers were James Alstad, Edson Asaga, David Beck, Earl Beede, Mack Bishop, William Blackburn, Edward Bodfish, Jorge Boria, Robert Burns, Adrian Carricart, John Chilenski, Douglas Clark, Lawrence Cox, Weidong Cui, Donald Dylla, Fedor Dzerjinski, Ralph Forey III, Eva Freund, Stephen Frezza, Jun Fukutomi, Pierce Gibbs, Thomas Glenn, Rebecca Grasser, Jill Hamada, Joel Henry, Karl Hoech, Bradey Honsinger, Pete Knoke , Stephen Masticola, Susan Mengel, Gilda Pour, Steven Roach, Edward Slosky, Jennifer Stuart, Andrey Terekhov, Karen Thurston, Edmundo Tovar, Michael Ulm, and Eric Yocam. This review process was complete by early 2003.

Later that year, Stephen Seidman and J. Fernando Naveda led a comprehensive problem review that was carried out by Heidi J. C. Ellis, Ann Gates, and James Moore. During a final meeting in Washington DC, Stephen Seidman, James Moore, Jenny Stuart, and J. Fernando Naveda compiled the final set of questions that were to be included in this book.

In 2004, we began the process of turning the sample questions into this book. We were greatly aided in this effort by our area editors, Heidi J. C. Ellis, Susan K.

Land, John Reisner, and Paula Strawser. The editors rewrote and reformatted the questions and answers, and provided appropriate context and references.

Acknowledgments

We would like to thank all of those who participated in this project. First and foremost, we would like to thank our area editors for their work on organizing the problems and putting them into the appropriate contexts. We would also like to thank Allen Parrish for contributing some problems at a crucial stage of the effort.

Portions of the book manuscript were reviewed by Gregory W. Hislop, Heidi J. C. Ellis, Tom Hilburn, Natalia Juristo, Susan K. Land, John Reisner, and Paula Strawser. We are very grateful for their comments.

We would also like to thank Deborah Plummer and Angela Burgess of the IEEE Computer Society.

Finally, we'd like to thank Stacy Saul of the IEEE Computer Society staff for her consistent and invaluable support of this project.

J. Fernando Naveda would like to thank the faculty, staff, and students of RIT's department of software engineering for their inspiration, support, and encouragement over the years.

Though we have received help from numerous individuals, any errors contained in this book are our responsibility.

J. Fernando Naveda
Rochester, New York
September, 2005

Stephen B. Seidman
Newark, New Jersey
September, 2005

About this Book

This book is intended for several audiences: prospective takers of the IEEE Computer Society's Certified Software Development Professional (CSDP) examination, graduate students of software engineering, and software engineering professionals. The chapters of the book correspond to the topics covered by the examination: business practices and engineering economics, software requirements, software design, software construction, software testing, software maintenance, software configuration management, software engineering management, software engineering process, software engineering tools and methods, and software quality. The questions, answers, explanations, and references found in the book can also serve as a guide to students and professionals.

The CSDP examination is a cornerstone of the Society's long-term effort to improve the professionalism of software engineers. In this context, a brief history of CSDP may be of interest. The CSDP effort began in 1998, when Leonard Tripp, the Society's 1999 President, initiated a study of software engineering professional certification. The first step was to gather input from the professional community. To do so, Tripp organized a study that included surveys and discussions with potential certificate holders and with industry representatives, and followed up with a survey of a sample of its members. The results of all of these efforts suggested that there was a strong interest in certification.

Under the continuing leadership of Leonard Tripp, the Computer Society contracted with Chauncey Group International (CGI), a subsidiary of the Educational Testing Service, to develop a certification examination. In 1999, a group of software engineers met under the guidance of CGI to review and revise a draft listing of task and knowledge statements. After validation by a group of software engineers, final versions of the task and knowledge statements were produced. The knowledge statements were mapped to the *Guide to the Software Engineering Body of Knowledge* (SWEBOK) in 2004, and the task statements were mapped to ISO/IEC 12207. Test specifications were then developed from information derived from the job analysis. The specifications became the blueprint for defining the final content of the examination.

The specification of the examination consists of the following eleven categories:

1. Business practices and engineering economics
    A. Engineering economics
    B. Ethics
    C. Professional practice
    D. Standards

2. Software requirements
    A. Requirements engineering process
    B. Requirements elicitation
    C. Requirements analysis

    B. Software configuration identification

    C. Software configuration control

    D. Software configuration status accounting

    E. Software configuration auditing

    F. Software release management and delivery

8. Software engineering management
    A. Measurement
    B. Organizational management and coordination
    C. Initiation and scope definition
    D. Planning
    E. Software acquisition
    F. Enactment
    G. Risk management
    H. Review and evaluation
    I. Project close out
    J. Post-closure activities

9. Software engineering process
    A. Process infrastructure
    B. Process measurement
    C. Process definition
    D. Qualitative process analysis
    E. Process implementation and change

10. Software engineering tools and methods
    A. Management tools and methods
    B. Development tools and methods
    C. Maintenance tools and methods
    D. Support tools and methods

11. Software quality
    A. Software quality concepts
    B. Planning for software quality assurance and verification and validation
    C. Methods for software quality assurance and verification and validation
    D. Measurement applied to software quality assurance and verification and validation

These categories correspond to the eleven chapters of this book. In the CSDP specification, each category is divided into several subcategories that represent the topics covered on the examination. The subcategories corresponding to each chapter are listed under each category and on the first page of the corresponding chapter.

In 2000, test items were written, edited and approved by groups of software engineers trained in item development by CGI, who then edited the items for style, format, logic, and grammar. The items were then evaluated for clarity, conciseness, and conformance to the test specifications. CGI ensured that the examination was psychometrically valid and culturally appropriate. Later that year, approved items were assembled into two independent exams, which were reviewed by a test developer and by a group of software engineers.

In 2001, the approved test exams were pilot-tested by an appropriately chosen group of software engineers. A preliminary item analysis was done on the pilot-test data to detect any errors in the key and any potentially flawed items. These errors were reviewed and corrected. A workshop was subsequently conducted to determine the cut score for the examination. The second exam was then statistically equated to the first. At this time, the examination was officially ready for release.

As of the summer of 2005, there are more than 450 CSDP certificate holders. These individuals reside in many countries. The examination is managed by Computer Society staff and supervised by the Society's Professional Practices Committee.

The chapters of this book correspond to the eleven categories of the CSDP examination specification. Each chapter contains a number of questions; the distribution of questions across the chapters corresponds roughly to the category weightings used for the examination. Each question is assigned to a specific subcategory. Some questions can be associated with more than one subcategory; in this case, we have made what we feel is the best subcategory assignment. Our intention was not to provide complete coverage of all subcategories, but rather to present a wide variety of problems and problem types. For that reason, some subcategories do not have any questions assigned. The correct answer for each question is provided, along with the appropriate context and references to the literature.

The complexity of the questions contained in this book spans the six cognitive levels described in Bloom's taxonomy: *knowledge, understanding, application, analysis, synthesis,* and *evaluation.* Each question is designed to test the reader's understanding of software engineering concepts at one of the levels of abstraction in Bloom's taxonomy. Using Bloom's taxonomy and a framework, questions in the CSDP exam and in this book can be classified into two broad categories: direct questions and case study questions. Direct questions are designed to gauge the exam taker's knowledge of software engineering concepts that can be found in the literature. Direct questions are at the knowledge, understanding, and application levels in Bloom's taxonomy. Case study questions, on the other hand, require a much deeper understanding of software engineering concepts. They present the reader with a hypothetical situation and then ask the reader a question.

The questions on the CSDP examination and, consequently, those in this book are all of the multiple choice type. Each question presents the reader with four possible answers and only one of them is the right answer to the question.

Though the book is designed for potential candidates for CSDP certification, other readers can benefit from it as well. Those interested in preparing for the CSDP exam can systematically answer each of the questions contained in the book from cover to cover. Others however, might prefer to jump to a specific area of the book where they feel they need to exercise most. Software engineering graduate students can use the book as preparation for comprehensive graduate level exams.

TABLE OF CONTENTS

Area editor: Susan K. Land

I. Business practices and engineering economics

Question   Jane is very pleased with the work a supplier does for her company and has referred partner companies to this supplier. Wanting to show its gratitude, the supplier has offered to update Jane's home network at a discount. This would not be a problem if:

a)   The discount is part of a publicly offered campaign.

b)   The supplier signs a written contract with Jane.

c)   The supplier has done work for others at the company.

d)   Jane's manager has the same work done in his/her house.

Answer: a

Explanation

The Software Engineering Code of Ethics and Professional Practice was developed by a joint task force of members from the IEEE Computer Society and the Association for Computing Machinery (ACM). Version 5.2 of this document was approved and finalized in 1998. The Code describes the ethical and professional obligations of software engineers. Principles 4.04 and 4.05 of the Code of Ethics state that software engineers should "not engage in deceptive financial practices such as bribery, double billing, or other improper financial practices," and that they are to "disclose to all concerned parties those conflicts of interest that cannot reasonably be avoided or escaped." The supplier's offer raises a potential conflict of interest and could be regarded as a deceptive or improper financial practice. It is therefore in conflict with the Code.

References

1. IEEE-CS/ACM Joint Task Force on Software Engineering Ethics and Professional Practices, *Computer Society and ACM Approve Software Engineering Code of Ethics*, IEEE Computer Magazine, October 1999.

2. *Software Engineering Code of Ethics and Professional Practice*, IEEE Press, 1999.

Question The IEEE Code of Ethics allows you to accept a position for which you have no pertinent training or experience if:

    I.   *Your limitations are fully disclosed.*

    II.   *Appropriate training in the pertinent area is taken concurrently.*

    III.   *The position is in a field in which engineering decisions are well known.*

    IV.   *No conflict of interest is present.*

a)   I only.
b)   I and II only.
c)   I, II, and III only.
d)   I, II, III, and IV.

Answer: a

Explanation

The Software Engineering Code of Ethics and Professional Practice was developed by a joint task force of members from the IEEE Computer Society and the Association for Computing Machinery (ACM). Version 5.2 of this document was approved and finalized in 1998. The Code describes the ethical and professional obligations of software engineers.

Principle 2 of the IEEE-CS/ACM Software Engineering Code of Ethics and Professional Practice states that "software engineers shall act in a manner that is in the best interests of their client and employer, consistent with the public interest." This is amplified in section 2.01, which further states that software engineers shall "Provide service in their areas of competence, being honest and forthright about any limitations of their experience and education."

References

1. IEEE-CS/ACM Joint Task Force on Software Engineering Ethics and Professional Practices, *Computer Society and ACM Approve Software Engineering Code of Ethics*, IEEE Computer Magazine, October 1999.

2. *Software Engineering Code of Ethics and Professional Practice*, IEEE Press, 1999.

A project manager is assigned to a new client who needs a web interface and database for online ordering. After assessing the scope of work, the manager decides that three GUI designers would be sufficient, and that they should work at the client's site. The manager assigns the work to the first three people listed on the available staff sheet, knowing that each of them has less than two months experience at the company, but also knowing that company policy is to hire only personnel who have graduated from an accredited university with a BS degree in a computing science.

Question The list below shows four ethical principles taken from the Software Engineering Code of Ethics and Professional Practice. Which principles might the manager have violated?

> I. *Ensure good management for any project on which they work, including effective procedures for promotion of quality and reduction of risk.*
>
> II. *Assign work only after taking into account appropriate contributions of education and experience tempered with a desire to further that education and experience.*
>
> III. *Not unjustly prevent someone from taking a position for which that person is suitably qualified.*
>
> IV. *Ensure that software engineers are informed of standards before being held to them.*

a) I, III, and III only.
b) I and II only.
c) I, II, III, and IV.
d) II and III only.

Answer: b

Explanation

The Software Engineering Code of Ethics and Professional Practice was developed by a joint task force of members from the IEEE Computer Society and the Association for Computing Machinery (ACM). Version 5.2 of this document was approved and finalized in 1998. The Code describes the ethical and professional obligations of software engineers.

I and II are taken directly from the Code of Ethics and Professional Practices (Principles 5.01 and 5.04, respectively). The manager's behavior directly contravenes both of these principles, which are given below.

Principle 5.01: Ensure good management for any project on which they work, including effective procedures for promotion of quality and reduction of risk.

Principle 5.04: Assign work only after taking into account appropriate contributions of education and experience tempered with a desire to further that education and experience.

References

1. IEEE-CS/ACM Joint Task Force on Software Engineering Ethics and Professional Practices, *Computer Society and ACM Approve Software Engineering Code of Ethics*, IEEE Computer Magazine, October 1999.

2. *Software Engineering Code of Ethics and Professional Practice*, IEEE Press, 1999.

A project manager is assigned to a new client who needs a Web interface and database for online ordering. After assessing the scope of work, the manager decides that three GUI designers would be sufficient, and that they would work at the client's site. The manager assigns the work to the first three people listed on the available staff sheet, knowing that each of them has less than two months experience at the company, but also knowing that company policy is to hire only personnel who have graduated from an accredited university with a BS degree in a computing science.

Question The manager's decision is a potential violation of which of the following principles from the Software Engineering Code of Ethics and Professional Practice?

a) Ensure proper and achievable goals and objectives for any project on which they work or propose.

b) Ensure that any document upon which they rely has been approved, when required, by someone authorized to approve it.

c) Use the property of a client or employer only in ways properly authorized, and with the client's or employer's knowledge and consent.

d) Disclose to all concerned parties those conflicts of interest that cannot reasonably be avoided or escaped.

Answer: a

Explanation

The Software Engineering Code of Ethics and Professional Practice was developed by a joint task force of members from the IEEE Computer Society and the Association for Computing Machinery (ACM). Version 5.2 of this document was approved and finalized in 1998. The Code describes the ethical and professional obligations of software engineers.

The answer is (a) as stated specifically in Principle 3.02 of version 5.2 of the Code of Ethics and Professional Practice.

References

1. IEEE-CS/ACM Joint Task Force on Software Engineering Ethics and Professional Practices, *Computer Society and ACM Approve Software Engineering Code of Ethics*, IEEE Computer Magazine, October 1999.

2. *Software Engineering Code of Ethics and Professional Practice*, IEEE Press, 1999.

Question According to the Software Engineering Code of Ethics and Professional Practice, software engineers are expected, as appropriate, to:

    I.   *Help develop an organizational environment favorable to acting ethically.*

    II.   *Promote public knowledge of software engineering.*

    III. *Participate in professional organizations, meetings, and publications.*

    IV. *Encourage colleagues to adhere to the Software Engineering Code of Ethics and Professional Practice.*

    V.   *Give full credit to the work of others.*

a)   I, III, and IV only.

b)   I, III, and V only.

c)   I, III, IV, and V only.

d)   I, II, III, IV, and V.

Answer: d

Explanation

The ACM/IEEE-CS Software Engineering Code of Ethics and Professional Practice was developed by a joint task force of members from the IEEE Computer Society and the Association for Computing Machinery (ACM). Version 5.2 of this document was approved and finalized in 1998. The Code describes the ethical and professional obligations of software engineers [1]. Version 5.2 of the Code contains the following principles:

> Principle 1: Public
>
> Principle 2: Client and Employer
>
> Principle 3: Product
>
> Principle 4: Judgment
>
> Principle 5: Management
>
> Principle 6: Profession
>
> Principle 7: Colleagues
>
> Principle 8: Self

The choices given above specifically appear in the Code:

Principle 6.01: Help develop an organizational environment favorable to acting ethically.

Principle 6.02: Promote public knowledge of software engineering.

Principle 6.03: Extend software engineering knowledge by appropriate participation in professional organizations, meetings, and publications.

Principle 7.01: Encourage colleagues to adhere to this Code.

Principle 7.03: Credit fully the work of others and refrain from taking undue credit.

References

1. IEEE-CS/ACM Joint Task Force on Software Engineering Ethics and Professional Practices, *Computer Society and ACM Approve Software Engineering Code of Ethics*, IEEE Computer Magazine, October 1999.

2. *Software Engineering Code of Ethics and Professional Practice*, IEEE Press, 1999.

You have recently created a new software product that applies a unique method. You want to protect this unique method.

Question   Referring to the above scenario, what should be pursued?

a)   Copyright.
b)   Patent.
c)   Product Registration.
d)   Trademark.

Answer: b

Explanation

There are three types of protection that may be used as legal protection for intellectual property. These three types of protection are: copyright, patent, and trademark.

A copyright protects a work from being reproduced without the permission of the copyright holder. A copyright may be invoked to protect literary, musical, dramatic, artistic, architectural, audio, or audiovisual work. Copyright laws give authors exclusive rights, most notably the right to make copies. Copyrights now last for an author's lifetime plus 70 years.

A patent may be used to protect physical inventions along with the inventive processes for producing a physical product. A patent can be defined as "a government grant which confers on the inventor the right to exclude others from making, using, offering for sale, or selling the invention for what is now a period of 20 years, measured from the filing date of the patent application."

The United States Patent and Trademark Office (PTO) began granting process patents for selected business methods in the 1990s. Since that time, the U.S. Court of Appeals has upheld such patents. The Court stated that business methods were not different from other methods or processes that were traditionally eligible for patent protection.

The final form of legal protection for intellectual property objects is the trademark. A trademark is a word, phrase, or symbol that uniquely identifies a product or service. Trademarks are recognized when they are first used, or when they are registered with the Patent Office.

References

1. State Street Bank & Trust Co. v. Signature Financial Group, 149 F.3d 1368 (Fed. Cir. Jul. 23, 1998).

2. Spinello, R.A, *CyberEthics: Morality and Law in Cyberspace, 2nd ed.*, Jones and Bartlett, 2003.

3. William Fisher, *Business Method Patents Online*, March, 2000; available at: http://eon.law.harvard.edu/property00/patents.

Area editor: Paula Strawser

II. Software Requirements

The InsurePro company develops software to support the commercial insurance industry and currently has several insurance products under development. A new customer-support application is proposed to allow customers to view the status of claims online. The development team for InsurePro responsible for developing the online claims application is working with the Customer Service department to develop the user interfaces for the claims application. The development group proposes to begin by creating Web-based forms for all claims whereas the Customer Service department proposes that potential users be polled to determine the most frequent use of the online system.

Question To develop the user interface for the online claims application, which of the following approaches would be most appropriate?

    I.   *Polling users*

    II.   *Defining and classifying interactions*

    III. *Developing prototype online claim forms*

a)   I only
b)   I and II only
c)   III only
d)   II and III only

Answer: b

Explanation

The first step of requirements engineering is *inception*, or project startup. This step is most often driven by the identification of a business need. *Elicitation* follows, in which the customer is consulted to identify objectives, intended use, business rules, and products. Elicitation is followed by *elaboration*, i.e., constructing an analysis model of the system. Scenarios and use cases are common products of elaboration. *Negotiation* follows elaboration: it is often necessary to negotiate with the customer the scope of the requirements that results in a usable system at an affordable cost. Once the scope is negotiated, the next step is *specification* of the requirements. The specification may be a document, a collection of models or scenarios, a prototype, or some combination of these. Finally, *validation* of the requirements is performed by a review team of software engineers, customers, users, and other stakeholders. Polling users is part of elicitation. Defining and classifying interactions is part of elaboration. Developing prototype online claim forms is a software development activity rather than a requirements engineering activity.

Reference

1. Pressman, R, *Software Engineering: A Practitioner's Approach*, 6th ed., McGraw-Hill, 2005.

A software development team adopted a plan for determining the requirements for an application, which included the following:

1. Creation of an online survey requesting feedback on suggested capabilities and asking for input on desired features.
2. Construction of a document including all of the desired features identified by the survey.
3. Creation of an interface prototype.
4. Presentation of the interface to management.

Question Which of the following requirements engineering steps were completely omitted in the requirements engineering plan?

  I.   *Requirements elicitation*

  II.   *Requirements elaboration*

  III.   *Negotiation*

  IV.   *Requirements specification*

  V.   *Requirements validation*

a)   I and II only
b)   I and V only
c)   II and IV only
d)   II and III only

Answer: d

Explanation

The online survey is a technique for *requirements elicitation*. The document created from survey results and the prototypes of the user interface are products of *requirements specification*. Presenting the interface to management is part of *requirements validation*. The missing steps are *requirements elaboration* and *negotiation*. *Elaboration* is an analysis and modeling activity, driven by refining the models of user-system interaction. Scenarios and use cases are common products of elaboration. *Negotiation* involves reaching agreement with the customer on the scope of the requirements, resulting in a usable system at an affordable cost. Impacts on cost and schedule are estimated based on the elaborated requirements, and risks are identified and assessed as a basis for the negotiation.

Reference

1. Pressman, R., *Software Engineering: A Practitioner's Approach* 6th ed., McGraw-Hill, 2005.

Jo is gathering the requirements for a software-controlled furnace. After interviewing several users, Jo obtained the following requirements list:

R1.   Gas inlet valves should always be open when furnace is heating.
R2.   Heating stops when furnace temperature reaches 150°C.
R3.   Furnace temperature should increase gradually when heating.
R4.   The gas inlet valves should be closed when the temperature goes above 200°C.

Question   Which requirements defects can be identified in Jo's requirements list?

       I. Ambiguous

      II. Design dependent

     III. Incomplete

     IV. Unverifiable

a)   I only
b)   I and II only
c)   II and III only
d)   I, III and IV only

Answer: d

Explanation

The word "gradually" makes R3 *ambiguous* and *unverifiable*. An unambiguous, verifiable expression for the requirement would be, for example, "Furnace temperature should increase no more than 1°C/second when heating." Even better would be, "Furnace temperature should increase between 1°C/second and 2°C/second when heating." The set of requirements is also *incomplete*, because they do not explain what happens when the temperature is over 150°C (heating done) and 200°C (valve closing). We suppose valves remain open, but we cannot be sure about it because R4 may be a safety requirement, and unrelated to R1 or R1. In part, incompleteness is caused because R1 and R2 interact in a very subtle way.

Reference

1. Davis, A, *Software Requirements: Objects, Functions and States,* Prentice-Hall, 1993.

During a software development project two similar requirements defects were detected. One was detected in the requirements phase, and the other during the implementation phase.

Question   Which of the following statements is mostly likely to be true?

a)   The most expensive defect to correct is the one detected during the requirements phase.

b)   The most expensive defect to correct is the one detected during the implementation phase.

c)   The cost of fixing either defect will usually be similar.

d)   There is no relationship between the phase in which a defect is discovered and its repair cost.

Answer: b

Explanation

Empirical evidence shows that the cost to correct a defect found in the design is, in general, 2.5 to 5 times the cost of fixing a defect found during the requirements phase. Similarly, a defect found in coding costs 5 to 10 times as much, and a defect found during unit test costs 10 to 20 times as much to fix as a defect found in the requirements phase. The increase in relative cost per defect is steeper in the acceptance test (25 to 50) and maintenance (100 to 200) phases of the system life cycle. For more information, see section 1.3 of the reference cited below.

Reference

1. Davis, A, *Software Requirements: Objects, Functions and States,* Prentice-Hall, 1993.

Question   Which of the following techniques is NOT used for validating requirements?

a)   Prototyping
b)   Animation
c)   Paraphrasing
d)   Regression

Answer: d

Explanation

Loucopoulos describes requirements validation as an unstructured quality assurance process. Its objective is to assure that the requirements are consistent, complete, unambiguous, minimal, and non redundant. In this context, *minimal* requirements means requirements that are not over specified and that do not include design information. It is interesting to note that requirements can be validated, but not verified. There is no existing process for requirements verification, although requirements will be the basis for verification in subsequent phases of the software life cycle.

Prototyping, animation, and paraphrasing are all techniques that are effective in presenting the requirements in ways that users can readily understand. *Prototypes* are working models of parts of the system that can be used in requirements elicitation and specification activities, as well as in requirements validation. *Animation* has been used effectively in validation of real-time systems. The user can interactively change the state of an object and observe an animation of the effects. *Paraphrasing* might be used to explain the results of a complex computation, without presenting all the technical details and formulae.

Regression, on the other hand, is a software testing technique that assumes the existence of a reference baseline. Each new version of software is tested and results are examined for variations from the baseline results. Variations most often indicate undesirable side effects of a change introduced in the current version.

References

1. Loucopoulos, P. and V. Karakostas, *System Requirements Engineering*, McGraw-Hill, 1995.

2. Pressman, R., *Software Engineering: A Practitioner's Approach* 6th ed., McGraw-Hill, 2005.

Question   Which of the following statements is not a valid requirements specification?

a)   Software shall be written in C.

b)   Software shall respond to all requests within five seconds.

c)   Software shall be composed of the following twenty-three modules.

d)   Software shall use menu screens whenever it is communicating with the user.

Answer: c

Explanation

The software requirements specification (SRS) includes two types of requirements: behavioral and nonbehavioral. Behavioral requirements describe what the system does. Nonbehavioral requirements describe attributes of the system, for example, the "-ilities" (reliability, maintainability, etc.) or standards compliance requirements. The software requirements should not include project requirements, design information, or product assurance plans.

Answer (a) is a valid nonbehavioral requirement. Answers (b) and (d) are valid behavioral requirements. Answer (c) is a design statement describing the structure of the software.

References

1. Davis, A., *Software Requirements: Objects, Functions and States,* Prentice-Hall, 1993.

User requirements describe both functional and nonfunctional aspects of the system in a way that the users of the system can understand without having detailed technical knowledge. Natural language, forms, and simple intuitive diagrams are used to document user requirements.

Question   Natural language is typically used for user requirements specification for which of the following reasons?

a) Ease of understanding
b) It is unambiguous
c) It is precise
d) It eliminates misunderstanding among stakeholders

Answer: a

Explanation

Requirements written in natural language are easier to understand, and it is more likely that users and stakeholders will take the time to read and review them. However, natural language is neither precise nor unambiguous, and therefore open to interpretation. Two stakeholders may interpret a requirement in different ways. Ambiguity is inherent in any natural language. Moreover, as systems become more complex, it becomes more difficult to describe the behavior of the system in an unambiguous way. Many people also find it difficult to write clear and concise natural language.

Sommerville and Sawyer advocate the use of a short style guide to describe how requirements should be written. They recommend certain key attributes; for example, keeping sentences short, and expressing only a single requirement per sentence. The style guide should be included as criteria for requirements reviews.

References

1. Sommerville, I, *Software Engineering* 6th ed., Addison-Wesley, 2001.

2. Somerville, I. and Sawyer, P., *Requirements Engineering: A Good Practice Guide*, John Wiley & Sons, 1997.

3. Davis, A., *Software Requirements: Objects, Functions and States,* Prentice-Hall, 1993.

A systems requirements analyst is asked to review the following requirement:

"The system shall be able to store one thousand (1000) 16-bit records in memory."

Question Which of the following requirements attributes does this requirement meet?

> I. *Unambiguous*
>
> II. *Implementation Independent*
>
> III. *Validatable*

a) I only
b) II only
c) I and II only
d) I and III only

Answer: d

Explanation

IEEE Std 1233,1998 edition, states the following: "Each requirement should possess the following properties:

a) *Abstract*. Each requirement should be implementation independent.

b) *Unambiguous*. Each requirement should be stated in such a way so that it can be interpreted in only one way.

c) *Traceable*. For each requirement it should be feasible to determine a relationship between specific documented customer statement(s) of need and the specific statements in the definition of the system given in the SyRS as evidence of the source of a requirement.

d) *Validatable*. Each requirement should have the means to prove that the system satisfies the requirements."

The requirement is unambiguous and validatable but implies implementation details, e.g., "16-bit."

Reference

1. IEEE Std 1233, *IEEE Guide for Developing System Requirements Specifications, 1998 edition,* IEEE Computer Society, 1998.

Question Which of the following requirement types should *NOT* be included in a Software Requirements Specification?

a) Functional requirements
b) Performance requirements
c) Project requirements
d) Maintainability requirements

Answer: c

Explanation

The Software Requirements Specification (SRS) is intended to describe the external behavior of the software system. *Functional* or *behavioral* requirements describe the behavior of the future software product, and are included in the SRS.   The SRS also includes nonbehavioral requirements: for example, levels of efficiency, security, capacity, the "-ilities," etc. So, *performance requirements* are nonbehavioral requirements, as are *maintainability requirements*. *Project requirements*, like restrictions on budget or schedule do not describe the software system itself, but rather describe the resource management plan for building the system.   Project requirements should not be included in the Software Requirements Specification.

Reference

1. Davis, A., *Software Requirements: Objects, Functions and States,* Prentice-Hall, 1993.

Question Of the following, which are of principal concern to requirements management?

    I. Managing change to agreed-upon requirements

    II. Managing relationships among requirements

    III. Managing dependencies between requirements documents and other documents

a) I and II only
b) II and III only
c) I and III only
d) I, II, and III

Answer: d

Explanation

During the development of requirements for a system, existing requirements change and new requirements emerge. Changes to the agreed-to requirements must be managed to keep cost and schedule within bounds, and to meet the customer's needs and expectations. Traceability of the relationships among requirements, as well as dependencies between requirements and other system development artifacts, are needed to assess the impact of changing a requirement.

Reference

1. Somerville, I. and Sawyer, P., *Requirements Engineering: A Good Practice Guide*, John Wiley & Sons, 1997.

Question Which of the following best describes the requirements management process?

a) The measure of requirements quality is that they remain invariant over time

b) A proposed requirement, once rejected, should remain rejected

c) Change is inevitable; requirements management must accommodate change

d) A relational database should be used when tracking requirements

Answer: c

Explanation

During the development of requirements for a system, existing requirements change and new requirements emerge. The first principal concern of requirements management is managing the changes to agreed-upon requirements. Although requirements volatility is an important indicator of requirements quality, there is no expectation that requirements will remain invariant over time. Likewise, a change control process is implicit in managing requirements, but this does not prohibit reinstating previously rejected requirements. For example, consider the case in which a requirement initially rejected as too costly is reinstated as a security measure in response to a newly identified threat. Finally, whereas a database may be used in managing requirements, a decision to use such a special-purpose tool is based on weighing costs and benefits.

Reference

1. Somerville, I. and Sawyer, P., *Requirements Engineering: A Good Practice Guide*, John Wiley & Sons, 1997.

Question Which of the following are least likely to be appropriate candidates for inclusion in a Software Requirements Specification?

a) Design constraints
b) Delivery constraints
c) Functions to be performed
d) Performance characteristics

Answer: b

Explanation

Christensen and Thayer list five categories of requirements: functions, performance, external interfaces, design constraints, and quality attributes. They also state that the Software Requirements Specification should address only product requirements. Programmatic items that describe what the development team is to do, such as cost, schedule, and project processes and procedures, belong in other project documents. Delivery constraints are programmatic items, and should not be included in the Software Requirements Specification.

Reference

1. Christensen, M. and R. Thayer, *The Project Manager's Guide to Software Engineering's Best Practices*, IEEE Computer Society, 2001.

Question Which of the following should be included in the Software Requirements Specification?

a) Acceptance procedures
b) Delivery schedules
c) Quality attributes
d) Quality assurance procedures

Answer: c

Explanation

Christensen and Thayer list five categories of requirements: functions, performance, external interfaces, design constraints, and quality attributes. They also state that the Software Requirements Specification should address only product requirements. Programmatic items that describe what the development team is to do, such as cost, schedule, and project processes and procedures, belong in other project documents. Acceptance procedures and quality assurance procedures are project processes, and thus programmatic items. The delivery schedule is also a programmatic item. Quality attributes is the only one of the items above that should be included in the Software Requirements Specification.

References

1. Christensen, M. and R. Thayer, *The Project Manager's Guide to Software Engineering's Best Practices*, IEEE Computer Society, 2001.

Question   Which of the following diagramming techniques can be used for expressing timing requirements?

    I.   *Data flow diagrams*

    II. *Decision trees*

    III. *Petri nets*

    IV. *State charts/transition diagrams*

a)   I and III only

b)   II and IV only

c)   III and IV only

d)   II, III, and IV only

Answer: c

Explanation

Data flow diagrams, decision trees, Petri nets, and state diagrams are all examples of semiformal notations that can be used to specify requirements. Data flow diagrams are generally used for process-related requirements; although there is a sequence to these diagrams, there is no notation for timing. Decision trees are used to specify logical requirements; again, there is no notation for timing. Both Petri nets and state diagrams do address timing issues. Petri nets are abstract virtual machines used to model concurrency and timing relationships for time-critical applications. State diagrams are used to model the state changes and outputs of a specific object in response to external stimuli, which would include timing signals.

References

1. Christensen, M. and R. Thayer, *The Project Manager's Guide to Software Engineering's Best Practices*, IEEE Computer Society, 2001.

2. Davis, A., *Software Requirements: Objects, Functions and States*, Prentice-Hall, 1993.

Question Which of the following types of requirements can be counted by function points?

      I.   Database requirements

      II. User interaction requirements

      III. Reporting requirements

      IV. Reliability requirements

a)   I and III only

b)   I, III and IV only

c)   I, II and III only

d)   III and IV only

45

Answer: c

Explanation

Jones explains that the primary purpose of function points is to estimate the size of the software dealing with the *external* aspects of a software application: inputs, outputs, inquiries that users can make logical files maintained by the application, and interfaces to other applications. This clearly covers database requirements (files), and user interaction and reporting requirements (inquiries that users can make, inputs and outputs), all of which affect software size.

Pressman tells us that reliability – a system's capability, over time, to correctly deliver services – is one of six key quality attributes as defined in the ISO 9126 standard. Although there is an implicit relationship between reliability requirements and the effort required to build quality into the system, reliability requirements do not define countable external aspects of the application and are not counted for function points.

References

1. Jones, C., *Estimating Software Costs*, McGraw-Hill, 1998.

2. Pressman, R., *Software Engineering: A Practitioner's Approach*, 6th ed., McGraw-Hill, 2005.

The following requirement was identified for the construction of a CASE tool:

R3: The user will be able to move the different entities of a diagram in the screen grid. Initially, the grid will be off. A zoom option will be provided by the tools. The grid might be toggled between centimeters and inches.

Question What course of action should be taken to best facilitate requirement management and traceability?

a) Restate the requirement to remove ambiguity in the language.

b) Separate the requirement into a set of singular requirements.

c) Consult the stakeholder to clarify the incomplete requirement statement.

d) Consult the stakeholder to correct the accuracy of the requirement.

Answer: b

Explanation

The first step in transforming this requirement into a manageable, traceable form is to separate it into distinct identifiable statements. The first sentence addresses a user interface capability. The second and fourth sentences address a state and a capability of the grid, respectively. The third sentence refers to a capability of "the tools."

Separating these sentences allows each statement to be analyzed separately. It is easier to detect ambiguities such as the "might be" language and the undefined (and therefore unverifiable) limits of the zoom capability. Restating the requirement may resolve the problem, or consulting the stakeholder may be required in order to correct the requirements.

Then the separate statements can be aggregated or associated with others that describe the same capability or characteristic or object: requirements that describe the grid, requirements that describe the capability of the user to manipulate entities of a diagram, general requirements for "the tools." It is then easier to analyze these related groups of requirements for completeness and consistency. Again, restating requirements, adding additional requirements, and consulting the stakeholder may be required to address requirements deficiencies.

Reference

1. Sommerville, I., *Software Engineering*, 6th ed., Addison-Wesley, 2001.

During the requirements validation process, two main problems were found in the requirements document created by analysts for a data conversion project:

- Maintainability of the specification, as requirements were specified in a way that was difficult to evolve;
- Verifiability, as some requirements were not easily demonstrable.

The requirements process took longer than planned, and as a consequence there was some delay in the project plan.

Question Which of the following actions is the project manager most likely to take?

a) Fix both problems before carrying on with the project.
b) Fix the verifiability problem and carry on with the project.
c) Fix the maintainability problem and carry on with the project.
d) Continue with the project and fix the problems during the design activity.

Answer: b

Explanation

Requirements validation assures that the requirements as specified meet the customer's needs. Design validation assures that the design meets the specified requirements. The validated design and requirements are the basis for implementation. The validated requirements are also the basis for system test. So the verifiability problem is important to all phases of system development, as well as to maintenance activities. The maintainability of the specification will have the greatest impact in the maintenance phase of the life cycle.

Fixing the verifiability problem will involve a careful review of the requirements and recasting those that are deemed unverifiable. Fixing the maintainability problem implies a restructuring of the specification, and perhaps even some investment in requirements management tools. Moreover, if the project is a one-time data conversion, maintainability of the specification may be moot.

Of course, one *should* choose to fix both problems, but this is not only likely to be cost-prohibitive, but also will introduce even more delay into the schedule. Continuing the project with the intent to fix problems in design activity introduces unacceptable risk; the design cannot be shown to conform to the requirements if the requirements are not verifiable. Fixing the maintainability problem but not the verifiability problem is clearly not acceptable. So the project manager will choose to fix the verifiability problem and proceed.

References

1. Pfleeger, S., *Software Engineering: Theory and Practice*, 2nd ed., Prentice-Hall, 2001.

You are a requirements engineer on a project that will replace the current training system for a large company's training department. The orientation process will be online rather than in a traditional setting, with a trainer and a group of new employees. Although some professional development courses will be offered online for use at the employee's leisure, other courses will be offered in a traditional mode, complemented with computer-based activities. The course-registration and payment systems will be revised to improve productivity through automation. The employee's department pays for the courses that the new employee needs to complete.

Question Which of the following is the STRONGEST argument for using the observation elicitation technique?

a) Direct one-on-one interaction with the user allows for an ongoing dialogue to discuss work patterns.

b) Observation allows one to see not only the normal workflow, but also the possibility to capture atypical situations.

c) Observation is the traditional approach for requirements gathering, and your company has experience using this technique.

d) Observation makes it easier for observers and subjects to interact more productively as they exchange ideas in real time.

Answer: b

Explanation

Robertson and Robertson describe the requirements analyst as a translator, who observes the work from the user's perspective to understand it. The requirements analyst then interprets the work while looking for patterns in the work. In this example, the analyst might be looking for patterns that would reveal those subjects best suited to online training, rather than a more traditional training mode. Robertson and Robertson also point out that users are very conscious of some requirements, and will bring them up early; but there are other requirements that are "second nature" to the user and that can only be discovered by observing the work. Sommerville describes a technique, "ethnography," that identifies implicit system requirements derived from observing the actual work performed; these include requirements imposed by the social and organizational context of the system.

Choice (a) above describes an interview technique rather than observation; observation is not as direct. It is not correct that observation is the traditional approach to requirements gathering; interview is more correctly regarded as "traditional." Also, the fact that a company has experience with observation is not in itself a strong argument; rather one would want to know how successful the company has been in the past using this technique. The assertion in choice (d) is questionable; observation may even make users nervous, making interaction more difficult.

References

1. Robertson, S. and Robertson J., *Mastering the Requirements Process*, Addison-Wesley, 1999.

2. Sommerville, I., *Software Engineering*, 6th ed., Addison-Wesley, 2001.

You are a requirements engineer on a project that will replace the current training system for a large company's training department. The orientation process will be online rather than in a traditional setting, with a trainer and a group of new employees. Although some professional development courses will be offered online for use at the employee's leisure, other courses will be offered in a traditional mode, complemented with computer-based activities. The course registration and payment systems will be revised to improve productivity through automation. The employee's department pays for the courses that the new employee needs to complete.

Your specific role on the project is as a requirements analyst.

Question   Which of the following is NOT a primary part of your role?

a)   While working with the users, the analyst observes their work and asks them questions about what they are doing and why they are doing it.

b)   The analyst interprets the information gathered from the users in order to better understand the essence of the work.

c)   The analyst is a domain expert who is a liaison between the users and the developers.

d)   The analyst invents a new work pattern that improves the work done by the user.

Answer: c

Explanation

Robertson and Robertson discuss the requirements elicitation process using a fishing metaphor – the analyst is "trawling" for requirements. They point out that the analysts have to understand the work the user currently does, as well as what the customer envisions the work to be in the future. Analysts observe the current work and interpret the information. They look for patterns. They develop an understanding of the fundamental reasons that the system exists: the "essence" of the system. Requirements analysts also look for improvements in existing work patterns, and they invent new work patterns to support future work.

Although a requirements analyst will learn a lot about the problem domain during the analysis, he/she will not become a domain expert. In this scenario, the users, trainers, and customers have the knowledge and experience; they are the domain experts.

References

1. Robertson, S. and Robertson, J., *Mastering the Requirements Process*, Addison-Wesley, 1999.

2. Sommerville, I., *Software Engineering*, 6th ed., Addison-Wesley, 2001.

You are a requirements engineer on a project that will replace the current training system for a large company's training department. The orientation process will be online rather than in a traditional setting, with a trainer and a group of new employees. Although some professional development courses will be offered online for use at the employee's leisure, other courses will be offered in a traditional mode, complemented with computer-based activities. The course registration and payment systems will be revised to improve productivity through automation. The employee's department pays for the courses that the new employee needs to complete.

Your organization has selected use cases as a requirements modeling tool.

Question Which of the following is NOT a characteristic of the application of use cases as a modeling tool?

a) Use cases present the functionality of the system in a stepwise fashion.

b) Use cases present the system from the user's point of view.

c) Each use case step can represent more than one requirement.

d) Use cases present the system from the system's point of view.

Answer: d

Explanation

Use cases are used to model the interactions between external entities, called "actors," and the system being modeled. The end user would be one of the actors in these models, so certainly the user's point of view is presented. The use case notation explicitly embodies the concept of sequence of interactions, and so presents functionality in a step-wise fashion. A use case may represent more than one requirement. The analyst may further elaborate the use case by adding scenarios for normal interaction as well as for exception conditions, or may represent further detail in a sequence diagram.

The system point of view might be documented as an architectural model. Other facets of the system point of view might be supported by a data flow model or an entity-relationship model. Use cases do not, however, present the system from a system point of view.

References

1. Robertson, S. and Robertson, J., *Mastering the Requirements Process*, Addison-Wesley, 1999.

2. Sommerville, I., *Software Engineering*, 6th ed., Addison-Wesley, 2001.

You are a requirements engineer on a project that will replace the current training system for a large company's training department. The orientation process will be online rather than in a traditional setting, with a trainer and a group of new employees. Although some professional development courses will be offered online for use at the employee's leisure, other courses will be offered in a traditional mode, complemented with computer-based activities. The course registration and payment systems will be revised to improve productivity through automation.

Jo, a novice requirements analyst, is overseeing the requirements engineering phase of the project. Jo has selected different models to present the system to the customer and developers. Virtually all of the effort is being dedicated to the functional requirements. The nonfunctional requirements are being neglected, and are considered to be unimportant.

Question   Which of the following is the STRONGEST argument for specifying the system's nonfunctional requirements?

a)   Nonfunctional requirements do not take as much time to specify as functional requirements.

b)   Nonfunctional requirements are not as important as functional requirements since features are what the customer requires from the system.

c)   Nonfunctional requirements are external characteristics of the product and they can always be factored in later on.

d)   Given that the functionality is present in the system, nonfunctional attributes determine how usable and useful the product is.

Answer: d

Explanation

Nonfunctional requirements define the customer's expectations of the qualitative behavior of the system. Some examples are: fast, easy to use, attractive, reliable, maintainable, portable, secure, and safe. These requirements are difficult to write because they must be quantitatively specified in order to be testable. What is the performance threshold for response time? What can we count that tells us a system is maintainable?

Also, if we build all the right functions but the user cannot learn how to use the system, we fail. The nonfunctional requirements cannot be factored in later, since they will be needed to complete the software architectural design of the system. Nonfunctional system features (often called "quality attributes") are often a consequence of decisions taken during software architectural design.

References

1. Robertson, S. and Robertson, J., *Mastering the Requirements Process*, Addison-Wesley, 1999.

2. Clements, P., Kazman, R., and Klein, M., *Evaluating Software Architecture: Methods and Case Studies*, Addison-Wesley, 2002.

You are a requirements engineer working on a project to develop a new racing game for a popular video game system. The game's features are based on the plot of an upcoming movie that your company has licensed the rights to use. The game's delivery date is to coincide with the release of the movie. Your organization has experience in developing educational games, but this genre is new. In order to gain market share in the gaming market, several recent college graduates have been hired as developers.

The movie studio wishes to view the game's requirements in order to provide an official game endorsement.

Question   Which of the following is the LEAST effective means for specifying the game's requirements?

a) Use cases
b) Activity diagrams
c) A prototype
d) Narrative format

Answer: d

Explanation

It is especially important in this case, in which the system is an interactive, fast-paced video game, that the requirements depict the action and the dynamics of the game. *Use cases* can be easily explained to the reviewers. Each use case, a combination of diagrams along with scenario scripts, describes how the user might interact with the system. For example, a use case might show how the user sets up the parameters of the game – character, difficulty level, special attributes, etc. *Activity diagrams* model the flow of activities for a particular class of objects. Decision nodes in these diagrams represent choices. For example, the possible sequences of actions that could occur when a character uses a particular kind of weapon can be modeled in an activity diagram. A *prototype* would be useful to illustrate the style of interaction between the user and the game, as well as showing graphics, sound, and color characteristics of the user interface.

A narrative description of the system is not always easy to follow and, since it is written in natural language, is open to ambiguity. It is also a static representation of the requirements in a case in which the dynamics of the game are all-important.

References

1. Leffingwell, D. and Widrig, D., *Managing Software Requirements: A Unified Approach*, Addison-Wesley, 2000.

2. Pfleeger, S., *Software Engineering: Theory and Practice, 2nd ed.*, Prentice Hall, 2001.

The Waterfall model is being followed to develop a computer game. The requirements passed inspection, and the design inspection was approved as accurately reflecting the game's requirements. During acceptance testing, one of the expert game players in the focus group found a defect that originated in the requirements. During analysis, the requirement was determined to be of low priority. The defect did not adversely affect the game play and was not fixed.

Question Which of the following is the strongest argument against fixing the requirement at this stage of development?

a) The cost of fixing the defect now is far more expensive than it would have cost to fix it earlier.

b) Since only a small percentage of game players are likely to notice, fixing the defect it is not worth the effort.

c) Since the game is not a critical domain application, defects found late in development are not usually fixed.

d) Since the likelihood of causing the failure is low, the defect is not a high priority.

Answer: b

Explanation

It is true that defects found in acceptance test are more expensive to fix – 30 to70 times more expensive – than defects found during the requirements phase. However, the change-control process takes into account not only cost, but also the severity of the defect, the probability of occurrence, and consequence of not fixing the defect. The change control board decision is made from a strategic and organizational point of view rather than a technical point of view. In this case, the defect did not adversely affect game play, and it is likely that most users would not even notice it.

If there were a defect in the game that adversely affected play, for example a defect that regularly crashed the game, it is likely that some remedial action would be taken and consequently some cost incurred. It is the impact of the defect on marketability that is important in this case, not the criticality of the application domain or the fact that defects at this stage are expensive to fix.

And although low probability of occurrence is an argument against fixing a defect, we are given no information in the problem statement on the likelihood that this particular defect will cause a failure.

References

1. Young, R., *Effective Requirements Practices*, Addison-Wesley, 2001.

2. Sommerville, I., *Software Engineering*, 6th ed., Addison-Wesley, 2001.

You are a requirements engineer working on a project to enhance a course-registration and payment system for a large public university system. Although you are new to the tasks needed to complete the project's requirements phase, you are asked to lead the team during the requirements elicitation phase.

Question You need to elicit requirements for the system. Which elicitation technique will BEST allow you to understand both the typical and atypical activities and tasks involved in course registration and payment?

a) Observation
b) Prototypes
c) Interviews
d) Questionnaires

Answer: a

Explanation

As in any requirements elicitation effort, a variety of methods and techniques will be used. But *observation* methods allow the best opportunity to uncover both typical and atypical requirements. Sommerville discusses an observational technique, ethnology, used to understand organizational and social requirements. This technique, he relates, can reveal critical process details that other techniques often miss. These include requirements derived from the way people actually perform their work (atypical) as opposed to the way the documented process describes the work being done (typical). The atypical requirements revealed by ethnology may also include requirements that are derived from cooperation between groups.

Prototypes, interviews, and questionnaires might be used along with ethnology. Most prototypes are developed quickly, either to get an initial sense of system requirements, or to explore less-understood areas of concern. Interviews tend to elicit the conscious, concrete requirements, but rarely address the more subtle implicit requirements. If the interviews are conducted according to a script, then the topics covered may be restricted to those identified in the script. Questionnaires are even more limited in scope, addressing only those items already known and included in the list of questions.

Reference

1. Sommerville, I., *Software Engineering*, 6th ed., Addison-Wesley, 2001.

You are a requirements engineer working on a project to enhance a course-registration and payment system for a large public university system. Although you are new to the tasks needed to complete the project's requirements phase, you are asked to lead the team during the requirements elicitation phase. The customer is continuously adding and changing requirements for the system despite a fixed delivery date.

Question What is the BEST argument for working with the customer to manage requirements?

a) The additional requirements will result in more coding work for the team which means the team will spend less time testing the system.

b) Functionality, cost, schedule, and quality are interrelated. Dialogue with the customer is required to achieve the appropriate trade-off.

c) The continuous revision to the requirements will hamper the verification, thus increasing the number of overall defects in the system and requiring more resources to test and remove them before delivery.

d) The inability to settle on requirements for some functions will likely reduce the scope of the product since the schedule is fixed.

Answer: b

Explanation

Although (a), (c) and (d) above are all possible consequences of failure to manage the requirements, only choice (b) addresses all the variables – cost, schedule, scope and quality – that must be considered in establishing the requirements baseline for the system. Leffingwell and Widrig remind us that it is, after all, the customer's business needs that should drive the trade-offs. The customer is the only party that can determine the scope of requirements that will result in a useful deliverable. Negotiating with the customer to establish the scope, estimating cost and schedule, and renegotiating the scope, if necessary, to meet the fixed cost and schedule requirements protects the customer from "surprises". Estimates should include adequate resources and time to assure the agreed-to level of quality for the system, so that necessary rework can be planned and managed within the project's budget and schedule.

Reference

1. Leffingwell, D. and Widrig, D., *Managing Software Requirements: A Unified Approach*, Addison-Wesley, 2000.

You are a requirements engineer working on a project to enhance a course-registration and payment system for a large public university system. You are the requirements analyst. You are also a recent university graduate, so you have experience in the problem domain. Consequently, less time is allocated for understanding the problem domain.

Question Which of the following is the MOST LIKELY consequence of conducting the requirements specification phase under these conditions?

a) Subtle mismatches between your conceptual understanding and the proper meaning of concepts within the domain are present, and will require rework.

b) The time saved during the elicitation process is allocated to the requirement validation process, where more defects can be detected.

c) Time is saved during the requirements specification process since you do not need to spend time asking follow-up questions to the stakeholders.

d) Mismatches in your conceptual understanding and the proper meaning are less likely to occur. The quality of the requirement specification is maximized.

Answer: a

Explanation

Van Vliet states, "Subtle mismatches between the analyst's notion of terms and concepts and their proper meaning within the domain being modeled can have profound effects. Such mismatches can most easily occur in domains we already 'know', such as a library." Such is the case here, the requirements analyst has experience in the problem domain.

It is unlikely that time will be saved during the requirements specification process, when the conceptual model of the system developed in requirements elicitation is documented. The time required to develop the specification is driven by size (number of requirements) and the choice of specification techniques. The domain knowledge of the analyst may shorten the requirements elicitation phase. And though it would be nice if the time "saved" were allocated to requirements validation, that is not likely to happen, and may not result in detecting more defects anyway. Requirements validation is in most cases an informal process, and the success depends on how well the users can understand the documented requirements. There is often a substantial amount of "translating" into the user's terms, with a consequent risk that defects will be missed, especially the subtle defects indicated in alternative (a).

References

1. Van Vliet, H, *Software Engineering: Principles and Practice*, 2nd ed., John Wiley & Sons, 2000.

You are a requirements engineer working on a project to enhance a course-registration and payment system for a large public university system. Although you are new to the tasks needed to complete the project's requirements phase, you are asked to lead the team during the requirements elicitation phase.

During the elicitation process, one of the requirements analysts interviews some students. The students tell the analyst all of the features that they want in the system. These features are subsequently added to the system's specification. During requirements analysis, the customer asks that some of the requirements proposed by the students be removed.

Question Which of the following is the WEAKEST argument for removing the students' requirements?

a) The students' requirements are not representative of the general student population.

b) The students' requirements are vague and not testable.

c) The students' requirements are contrary to the customer's interests.

d) The customer does not consider the students to be stakeholders in the system.

Answer: d

Explanation

The two main sources of requirements for a system are (1) the users, and (2) the problem domain. Users include both direct users, those who will interact directly with the system, and indirect users who consume information produced by the system. In the case of a course registration system, the students are direct users, and therefore very important stakeholders. So, argument (d) is patently absurd.

If the students' requirements are not representative, or they are vague and unverifiable, then the fault lies with the requirements elicitation process. Until the ambiguities are eliminated and the requirements understood, it would be difficult to make a reasonable case for removing the requirements in question.

Some of the students' requirements may indeed be "contrary" to the customer's interests if the cost of implementation is too high. These would be items for the *Negotiation* phase that Pressman describes, between the requirements elicitation and the requirements specification phases.

References

1. Van Vliet, H, *Software Engineering: Principles and Practice*, 2nd ed., John Wiley & Sons, 2000.

2. Pressman, R., *Software Engineering A Practitioner's Approach* 6th ed., McGraw-Hill, 2005.

An organization has gathered and analyzed requirements from the stakeholders for a new project, "Video Editing Software for the Hobbyist." The organization has experience with developing software, but not with commercial off-the-shelf software titles. The development team consists of thirty people with varying levels of experience. During the requirements phase, the team noticed that the source of each requirement is documented by the name of the person who first presented the requirement and the date gathered.

Question   Which missing pieces of information will have the GREATEST IMPACT on the analysis task required during change management?

   I.   *Traceability*

   II.   *Requirement Type*

   III.   *Priority*

   IV.   *Source*

a)   I and II only
b)   II and IV only
c)   I and III only
d)   III and IV only

Answer: c

Explanation

Several pieces of information are used to evaluate a proposal to change a given requirement. The *priority* of the proposed change reflects the importance or criticality of the request. In most prioritization schemes, a priority 1 change identifies a safety or security hazard and takes precedence over all other changes, whereas a priority 4 or 5 change is "nice to have." Priority is a key piece of information needed to make the yes/no decision and allocate the requirement to a specific release or software version. In addition, the cost and schedule impact of the requested change is key information. *Traceability* information contributes to impact analysis; it is the key to identifying all affected components. Other information needed to evaluate a change request might include technical feasibility/risk or analysis of alignment with the project's objectives and resource constraints. It is unlikely that the requirement type alone will have a great impact, although business objectives might favor, for example, increased performance over enhanced functionality. The source of the requirement is not missing.

References

1. Wiegers, K., *Software Requirements,* Microsoft Press, 1999.

2. Sommerville, I., *Software Engineering*, 6th ed., Addison-Wesley, 2001.

An organization has gathered and analyzed requirements from the stakeholders for a new project, "Video Editing Software for the Hobbyist." The organization has experience with developing software, but not with commercial off-the-shelf software titles. The development team consists of thirty people with varying levels of experience.

During requirements elicitation, the organization needed to get input from many users. After the initial requirements gathering activity, some video hobbyists were selected for in-depth interviews.

Question Which of the following is the MOST EFFECTIVE technique for the initial requirements elicitation?

a) The observation of parents videotaping their children playing in a local soccer game

b) The distribution of questionnaires at a consumer electronics store, which also sells software

c) A facilitated meeting of employees who engage in video editing at the company

d) The observation of parents shopping for software at a local computer store

Answer: b

Explanation

This organization needs to do a broad market survey of the video editing features most in demand by home editing enthusiasts in order to have a sound basis for its first venture into commercial off-the-shelf software. The most efficient instrument for reaching large numbers of people is a questionnaire. Although the questionnaire is passive, not allowing interaction with the respondent, a well-designed questionnaire can yield useful information from large numbers of potential customers. Questions that ask the responder to rate or rank services and features, for example, would be useful in determining the set of requirements allocated to the first version of the product.

Observing parents videotaping their children would reveal little about what editing might later be needed, although it would almost certainly validate a need for editing. A facilitated meeting of employees might be useful in designing a questionnaire, but the group would likely not be representative of the wider market and that could introduce bias. Observing parents shopping for software might yield some information about the relative popularity of existing editing software, but this kind of information can be garnered from other, more reliable sources.

References

1. Maciaszek, L., *Requirements Analysis and System Design: Developing Information Systems with UML*, Addison-Wesley, 2001.

An organization has gathered and analyzed requirements from the stakeholders for a new project, "Video Editing Software for the Hobbyist." The organization has experience with developing software, but not with commercial off-the-shelf software titles. The development team consists of thirty people with varying levels of experience. Instead of building the new system as a new product, the software organization decided to build it as an update from an existing product. As the requirements review is being planned, management has indicated that a more rigorous inspection is desired, although the organization's previous practice had been to conduct an ad-hoc requirements review.

Question Which of the following is *not* an appropriate party to include in the inspection team?

a) The requirements analyst who authored the document being reviewed
b) The project manager
c) A member of the test team
d) A system architect with experience on the previous release of the system

Answer: b

Explanation

Participants in the inspection should represent three perspectives: the author of the requirements, the author of any predecessor work product, and people who do work based on the reviewed requirements. The system architect represents the second perspective, and the test team member the third. The inspection focuses on technical issues, and the manager of a 30-person team is unlikely to have the time or need to acquire deep technical knowledge in the subject area. It would therefore not be appropriate to include him/her in the inspection team.

Reference

1. Wiegers, K., *Software Requirements,* Microsoft Press, 1999.

An organization has gathered and analyzed requirements from the stakeholders for a new project, "Video Editing Software for the Hobbyist." The organization has experience with developing software, but not with commercial off-the-shelf software titles. The development team consists of thirty people with varying levels of experience.

During the requirements inspection phase, the requirements are evaluated for verifiability.

Question Which of the following requirements is MOST LIKELY to be verifiable?

a) The EZ-Edit user interface will be easy to use by the novice-level computer user.

b) When required, EZ-Edit will automatically recognize supported video cameras and begin downloading video.

c) The compression scheme used to store video on the hard drive will minimize the size of the video file.

d) The size of the EZ-Edit application, with supporting files, will fit on a 1.44 megabyte diskette.

Answer: d

Explanation

In (a), "easy to use" is not quantifiable, nor is "novice user." "Novice user" might be better defined as one who is familiar with the target environment but not with video editors. "Easy to use" might be defined in terms of the minimum number of editing functions a new user should be able to exercise immediately after an interactive tutorial session.

In (b), the phrase "when required" is ambiguous. The real requirement might be that when a supported video camera is connected to the system, EZ-Edit will prepare to download video and prompt the user for confirmation. This is probably still not sufficient, as there are two cases: the camera is connected while EZ-Edit is running; the camera is connected before EZ-Edit is started. More important, whether the device can be detected by the software depends on the capabilities of the operating system in the target environment.

In (c), "minimize" is not testable. The requirement would be better stated as a minimum percent reduction from the uncompressed file size, and, of course, there are considerations such as preserving image quality and commercial compression schemes that would apply as well.

We can easily test (d) by copying the application and supporting files onto a 1.44 megabytes diskette.

Reference

1. Young, R., *Effective Requirements Practices*, Addison-Wesley, 2001.

Area editor: Heidi J. C. Ellis

III.   *Software Design*

1	III	SOFTWARE DESIGN	
	A		Software design concepts

Question What type of relationship would exist between the classes Account and Customer if each Customer may own any number of Accounts (zero, one, or more) and each Account may be owned by any number of Customers?

a) One-to-one

b) One-to-many

c) Many-to-many

d) Zero-to-many

Answer: c

Explanation

A many-to-many relationship is a relationship between two state classes in which each instance of one class may be associated with any number of instances of a second class (possibly none), and each instance of the second class may be related to any number of instances of the first class (possibly none). Since the problem description of the `Account` and `Customer` class relationship specifically states that instances of either class may be related to zero or more instances of the other class, the relationship between the `Account` and `Customer` classes is a many-to-many relationship.

Answer (a): A one-to-one relationship is a relationship between two classes in which each instance of one class may be associated with only a single instance of a second class (possibly none), and each instance of the second class may be related to only a single instance of the first class (possibly none). Since in the `Account` and `Customer` example, each `Account` instance may be associated with more than a single instance of a `Customer`, and each `Customer` instance may be associated with more than a single instance of an `Account`, the relationship is not a one-to-one relationship.

Answer (b): A one-to-many relationship is a relationship between two classes in which each instance of one class, referred to as the *child* class, is restricted to relating to no more than one instance of a second class, called the *parent* class. Each instance of the parent class may be associated with zero or more instances of the child class. In the `Account` and `Customer` example, neither `Account` instances nor `Customer` instances are specifically constrained to relate to no more than a single instance of the other. Therefore the relationship between the `Account` and `Customer` classes is not a one-to-many relationship.

Answer (d): A zero-to-many is not a valid relationship type. A relationship represents a connection between two, not necessarily distinct, classes. Therefore, a relationship must include two participating classes.

References

1. IEEE Std 1320.2-1998, IEEE Standard for Conceptual Modeling Language Syntax and Semantics for IDEF1X97 (IDEF object), section 5.5.1.

A new engineer has been assigned to an eight-person project team. Four developers assigned to the project have been creating designs and coding together for years. The current project is 3 months into construction, and another 6 months of construction are expected. The new engineer discovers that the design documentation is somewhat limited but acceptable, although there seem to be inconsistencies between the design document and the requirements. The code is a disappointment, being poorly documented, inconsistent, and making use of some questionable techniques. The team is willing to revisit the design documentation and expand it, but isn't interested in changing coding practices.

Question The WEAKEST of the following arguments for increasing code quality is:

a) The project is only a third of the way toward completion, so increasing code maintainability will increase future efficiency.

b) The company's coding standard dictates specific code practices.

c) Consistency across the code base will reduce the chance of defects being injected.

d) Better written code could reduce the need to expand design documentation.

Answer: d

Explanation

When evaluating all four answers, the improvement of the design documentation has the least impact on the final project outcome of the four answers provided. The quality of the code has only a marginal impact on the design documentation and improving the quality of the code will not make up for deficits in the design documentation. Better written code does not imply that the code is self-documenting. Furthermore, code documentation need neither imply nor include design documentation.

Increasing code quality will increase the maintainability of the project, which will have a strong positive effect on future efficiency. Since estimates of the cost of maintenance range from 50% to 75% of the total cost of a project, emphasis on the maintainability of the code will reduce development costs in the future. Given that keeping the cost of a project within budget is a primary constraint in most commercial development efforts, increasing maintainability of the project is a compelling reason to improve code quality, not a weak reason. This eliminates (a) as a possible answer.

Coding standards embody the company's philosophy and approach to design and development and therefore serve as a consistent base of understanding for the project. Coding practices impact the readability, understandability, and maintainability of the code. Since all of these factors directly impact development time and cost, requiring developers to follow the company's coding standard is another strong reason for supporting changing the coding practices. Thus, (b) is not the answer we are looking for.

Since the injection of defects at the coding stage will likely increase development time and cost, answer (c) is also a strong reason for the project team to change coding practices. The later in development that defects are detected, the more costly they are to remove. Since ensuring consistency across the code base will reduce the number of defects being introduced into the code, fewer defects will be passed along to the testing phase. A fewer number of defects will reduce testing time and increase efficiency of project development. Answer (c) is therefore another strong reason to change the development team's coding practices.

Since answers (a) through (c) are all strong reasons to change the coding practices, and since higher-quality code would only minimally reduce the need to expand the design documentation and minimally impact both the time and cost of development, answer (d) is the weakest reason for changing coding practices.

Reference

1. Sommerville, I., *Software Engineering*, 6th ed., Addison-Wesley, 2001.

After the requirements phase for the XYZ project, the design team was given additional time beyond the original plan to develop a complete object-oriented class model. This model was documented with a drawing tool in a large hierarchy of highly detailed UML class diagrams. The project moved into the construction phase utilizing reviews to ensure the consistency of the code, with the design and automated unit tests providing 100% public interface coverage for all classes. Approximately 20% of the way through implementation of the classes, enough functionality was in place to allow for system testing to start on the first vertical slice of functionality. The initial system testing went almost flawlessly. The review process and unit testing were completed. As more functionality was added to the system, however, system testing uncovered an unusually large number of problems related to object lifetimes, communication between objects, and synchronization. By the time 50% of the class model was implemented, the project manager was worried that the project was spiraling toward infinite defect mode.

Question   Which of the following design techniques would have been likely to produce a reduction in the problems that the project is facing:

      I.   State diagrams

     II.   Collaboration/Sequence diagrams

    III.   Entity-Relation Diagrams

    IV.   Activity diagrams

    V.   Package diagrams

a)   I, II and IV only
b)   II and IV only
c)   II, IV and V only
d)   I and III only

Answer: a

Explanation

The problems identified in the description; object lifetimes, communication between objects, and synchronization; are all problems related to the dynamic behavior of the XYZ project. State, collaboration/sequence, and activity diagrams are key views of this dynamic behavior that would allow for early modeling, which can help alleviate the problems the project is experiencing. Therefore, the correct answer that includes all listed design techniques that model the dynamic behavior is answer (a). Note that package diagrams and entity-relation diagrams, though providing useful static views of the software system, do not provide enough help in addressing the problems the system is having.

State diagrams are used for modeling the dynamic portions of a system at the object level. State diagrams show all possible states that objects in a system under design may be in, as well as showing how each object changes state as a result of events that affect the object. State diagrams show the lifetime behavior for a single object in a system and the behavior of a system may be described by creating state diagrams for every object in the system.

Collaborations are collections of classes, interfaces and other system elements that work together to supply a behavior that is too large to be provided by a single class or interface. Collaboration diagrams are a form of UML interaction diagrams that describe both static and dynamic aspects of a system at a somewhat higher level than state diagrams. Collaboration diagrams depict the classes, interfaces and other elements involved in the collaboration, and show how they interact to accomplish a task via an ordered sequence of messages sent for a given use case for the collaboration.

Sequence diagrams are one of the five types of UML diagrams that are used to model the dynamic aspects of a system. Specifically, sequence diagrams show the interaction of a series of objects, including a time ordering of the messages passed among the objects. Sequence diagrams differ from collaboration diagrams in that they depict the lifetime of the objects involved in the interaction, as well as having a focus of control that indicates the period of time in which an object is performing an action.

Entity-relation diagrams are used to model the data objects in a system and their relationships to one another. The goal of entity-relation diagrams is to accurately model the data used by the system and show how the data is statically related. Entity-relation diagrams contain no behavior specification and are frequently used in database design.

Activity diagrams are one of the five types of diagrams used in UML for modeling dynamic system behavior. Activity diagrams model the sequential steps in a computational process and are used to model flow of control. The primary form of activity diagrams is a flowchart. Activity diagrams focus on the flow of control between activities whereas sequence diagrams focus on the flow of activities between objects. Activity diagrams may also be used to model concurrent processes.

Package diagrams show how classes are grouped together to form higher-level units and the dependencies between these units. Package diagrams are a form of class diagram and therefore present a static view of the system. Although package diagrams help with decomposition complexity, they do not provide any insight into the dynamic behavior of the system.

From the descriptions above, state diagrams, collaboration/sequence diagrams and activity diagrams all provide dynamic perspectives on system design, whereas the entity-relation and package diagrams provide static views of a system. Since the problems in the development of the XYZ system revolve around object lifetimes, communication between objects, and synchronization, the only answer that includes all diagrams that depict the dynamic behavior of the system is answer (a).

References

1. Fowler, M, *UML Distilled: A Brief Guide to the Universal Modeling Language*, 2nd ed., Addison-Wesley, 2000.

2. Booch, G., J. Rumbaugh, and I. Jacobson, *The Unified Modeling Language User Guide*, Addison-Wesley, 1999.

The design for the XYZ project consisted of a comprehensive static view of the system captured in a drawing tool as a highly detailed set of UML class diagrams. The project moved into the construction phase, utilizing reviews to ensure the consistency of the code with the design, and automated unit tests providing 100% public interface coverage for all classes.

The initial system testing for the project went almost flawlessly. However, as more functionality was added, system testing uncovered more and more problems related to object lifetimes, communication between objects, and synchronization. By the time 50% of the class model was implemented, the project manager was worried that project was spiraling toward infinite defect mode.

Question   What is the most likely design process flaw this project is facing?

a) Use of object-oriented design

b) Not using a CASE tool to manage the class model

c) Insufficient design views

d) Insufficient time spent on class design

Answer: c

Explanation

The IEEE 1016-1998 IEEE Recommended Practice for Software Design Descriptions states that the software design description is a model of the system to be created and indicates that design information be organized into a variety of *design views*. Each design view provides a different perspective or viewpoint of the system and represents a different concern of the system. In order to comprehensively model a system, design views must capture both the static and dynamic properties of the system under development. The problem description clearly states that the static class model was the only type of design view developed for the project. All of the problems the project is encountering stem from dynamic behavior. Since modeling did not capture the dynamic behavior of the system, additional design views should be constructed to capture this information.

Answer (a): The use of object-oriented design would not necessarily aid in the design of the behavioral aspects of the system. In fact, the use of UML described in the problem description implies that an object-oriented design approach may have been used and the developers still neglected to model the dynamic portions of the system. Therefore, the use of an object-oriented design approach alone would not fix the problems related to the dynamic system behavior.

Answer (b): The problem statement indicates that a drawing tool was used to capture the UML class diagrams. The use of a more advanced CASE tool to manage the class model would possibly have allowed the class model to be more easily created, modified and understood. However, the use of a CASE tool in itself would not provide the additional dynamic views of system behavior needed to capture system behavior.

Answer (d): Additional time spent on class design may or may not have uncovered the fact that the behavior of the system was inadequately described by the sole use of class diagrams. The time spent on designing the XYZ project should have been more equally distributed across both the static and dynamic views of the system. Indeed, designing the dynamic portions of the XYZ project would have added effort. However, the case study strongly hints that design was not rushed in any way, and that sufficient time was spent to capture the range of system features. Therefore, spending more time on class design would not be sufficient to qualify answer (d) as the best answer to the question, as the real problem is not insufficient time but insufficient design views.

References

1. IEEE 1016-1998, *IEEE Recommended Practice for Software Design Descriptions*, Section 6.2.

The software development organization Fabulousoft is going to develop a software system for a bank. The system will be used by bank cashiers to serve customer requests. The efficiency of the cashier using the software product is critical for the success of the project. The bank has a high turnover rate for bank cashiers. A hard requirement from the bank, based on standard industry practice, is that their cashiers should be able to enter 80% of the operations into the system in less than a minute for each client.

Question   Which of the following approaches is the best to develop a software product that meets this usability requirement?

a)   Develop the internal part of the system first, and then give it to the human factors experts so they can provide the system with a highly usable user interface.

b)   Develop a highly efficient system in terms of internal data processing, and then provide the client with an intensive training program for the bank cashiers.

c)   Study the characteristics of the bank cashiers and the tasks they currently perform as a first step, and then perform iterative design on the system complemented with usability tests with real bank cashiers, until the usability goals are met.

d)   Clarify beforehand that this requirement is not feasible, and therefore Fabulousoft will decline to develop this product if the bank insists on including it as requirement.

Answer: c

Explanation

Usability is considered to be the degree to which a software system, and the user interface in particular, support the effective and efficient completion of a set of tasks within a context. Usability engineering is an approach to user interface development that uses a variety of structured methods for achieving usability during product development. Such structured methods incorporate key principles that include early focus on users and tasks, empirical measurement, and an iterative design process that incorporates user feedback.

Answer (a) proposes that the user interface be developed after the system internals have been designed. However, a key tenet of usability engineering is the early incorporation of users in the development process. Delaying user involvement until after system internals have been designed may result in a system with low usability or dissonance between the user interface and internal system structure. Therefore, developing system internals before designing the user interface is likely to result in software with low usability. Therefore (a) cannot be the answer.

Since the requirement that cashiers be able to enter 80% of the operations into the system in less than a minute for each client is a hard requirement, system usability should take precedence over internal efficiency. In addition, a less usable system will result in higher training requirements for new users. Since there is a high turnover rate for cashiers in the bank, developing a system that requires an intensive training process for new employees would result in higher costs in the long term. Therefore, (b) is not the answer we are looking for.

Answer (c) is the only answer that incorporates the three main tenets of usability engineering: early focus on users and tasks, empirical measurement, and an iterative design process that incorporates user feedback. Therefore, answer c describes the best approach to developing a software product that meets the usability requirements as described in the problem statement.

Answer (d) suggests that the usability requirements of this application are not feasible. However, Usability engineering techniques can easily handle the usability requirements included in the problem description. Therefore, there is no need for Fabulousoft to either require the usability requirement to be changed or to decline the development of the product.

Reference

1. Mayhew, D.J., *The Usability Engineering Lifecycle: A Practitioner's Handbook for User Interface Design*, Morgan Kaufmann Publishers, 1999.

The diagrams shown below, together with the explanations of the two events labeled "E-1" and "E-2," describe a warehouse's data flow using Yourdon's Modern Structural Analysis.

Event	Description
E-1:	**Customer sends orders daily.** **Customer receives supplies according to orders.** **When warehouse runs out of stock, orders are filed**
E-2:	**Filed orders are processed when supplier has enough items in stock.**

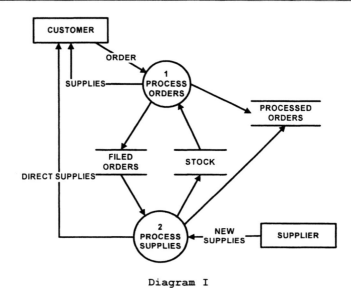

Diagram I

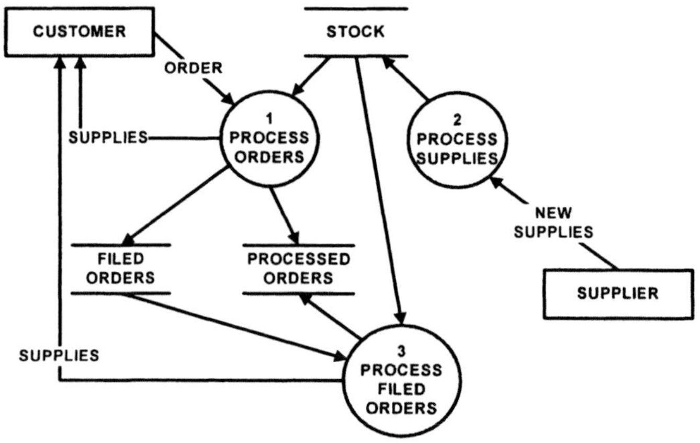

Diagram II

Question Disregarding syntactical matters, which of the statements below is true?

a) Only diagram I is correct.
b) Only diagram II is correct.
c) Diagrams I and II are both correct.
d) Neither diagram is correct.

Answer: a

Explanation

When using Modern Structural Analysis in a data flow diagram obtained from the event list, the boxes represent the actors in the system and the circles represent processes. Each circle has a name that represents the system's response to the associated event. Inputs and outputs are identified as arrows into or out of the circle. Data stores show required information used by the process. An event is modeled via an arrow from an actor to a process labeled with the event. Additionally, an event is defined as a beginning-to-end transaction. In this example, there are two events: the customer places an order (Order) and the supplier provides new supplies (New supplies). A correct diagram should have one and only one process circle for each event. This situation of a begin-to-end transaction modeled using a single process circle for each event is correctly shown in Diagram I. However, the functionality in Diagram II that supports the "New supplies" event is split into two processes (2 and 3). Therefore, the only correct diagram is Diagram I and the correct answer is (a).

Reference

1. Yourdon, E., *Modern Structured Analysis*, Prentice-Hall, 1989.

Question   In Modern Structured Analysis, the "event list" is used to:

a)   Improve requirements traceability
b)   Build an entity-life history diagram
c)   Document the data transactions in the entity-relationship diagram
d)   Build a preliminary data flow diagram for the system

Answer: d

Explanation

The event list in Modern Structured Analysis is a list of the events in the system environment to which the system must respond. The event list is used to produce a data flow diagram (DFD) for the system as part of the process of constructing a preliminary behavioral model of the system. The construction of the DFD begins by creating a circle for every event on the event list and labeling it with an event name. Inputs, outputs, and data stores are then added. Last, the high-level DFD is verified against the context diagram and event list for completeness and consistency.

The event list defines the events in the system that should come from the requirements. However, the event list is a simple, textual list of the events and the events on the list are not related to the requirements document in any formal fashion. Therefore, the event list is not related to improving the traceability of the requirements in the system and answer (a) is incorrect.

The entity-life history diagram is a comprehensive representation of the order in which processes operate on data and the number of times a particular process is carried out. Data flow diagrams do not contain any sequencing or iteration information whereas the entity-life history provides a description of the behavior of a system. In addition, entity-life history diagrams are part of the Structured Systems Analysis and Design Method (SSADM), not Modern Structured Analysis; therefore answer (b) is incorrect.

The entity-relationship diagram (ERD) depicts the information contained within a system and the relationships between the data. Although the nouns in the event list may be useful for identifying the objects in the ERD, the ERD is a static diagram and does not contain information about actions or events. Therefore, the event list is not used to document any part of the ERD, and answer (c) is incorrect.

The preliminary Data Flow Diagram for a system is constructed directly from the event list. Therefore, answer (d) is the correct answer.

Reference

1. Yourdon, E. *Modern Structured Analysis*, Prentice-Hall, 1989.

Question When using Yourdon's structured analysis method, in which order should the main design diagrams (data flow and entity-relationship) be constructed?

a) Entity-relationship then data flow

b) Data flow then entity-relationship

c) Both concurrently

d) It does not matter

Answer: c

Explanation

When using Yourdon's structured analysis, initial versions of the entity-relationship diagram (ERD) and the data flow diagram (DFD) should be developed independently and in parallel with each other. These two diagrams may be used to verify each other. For instance, the data stores identified in the DFD suggest the entities that should be contained in the ERD, and the objects identified in the ERD may help identify stores in the initial DFD. The views of the system provided by the DFD and the ERD must be consistent and compatible with one another. Creating the ERD before the DFD will bias the development of the latter. Therefore answer (a) is incorrect.

Likewise, creating the DFD before the ERD will tend to bias the development of the latter. Therefore, answer (b) is incorrect.

Both diagrams must be constructed concurrently. In addition, each diagram should be used to provide design assistance to the other. Therefore, answer (c) is correct.

If either diagram is completed before the other, one of the diagrams may bias the construction of the other. In addition, it will be more difficult to ensure that the views of the ERDs and DFDs are consistent and compatible with each other if they are developed in a sequential fashion. The best approach is to develop both diagrams in parallel. Therefore, answer (d) is incorrect.

Reference

1. Yourdon, E. *Modern Structured Analysis*, Prentice-Hall, 1989.

Question In structured design, why are afferent and efferent flows identified when performing transform analysis?

a) The flows represent data internal to the system.

b) The flows are limited by the physical constraints of the devices.

c) The system design should be independent of the format of the data.

d) The system performance depends mainly on the time of the flows.

Answer: c

Explanation

Transform analysis is one of two ways of deriving a structured chart from a Data flow diagram (DFD) using Structured Design. In transform analysis, the DFD is examined to partition the processes into those that perform input and editing, those that perform processing or data transformation, and those that perform output. The part of the DFD related to the processes that perform input and editing are referred to as the *afferent flows*. Central transform is used to refer to the processes that process or transform the data whereas the term *efferent flows* is used to refer to the part of the DFD that performs output. These afferent and efferent flows represent physically dependent data, produced by the input devices or consumed by the output devices. The system design should be as independent as possible of this kind of data, because the I/O devices may require different data formats. The output of Transform analysis is a structure chart that graphically illustrates a modular design of a program. Structure charts show the partitioning of a program into modules and the organization and communication between the modules.

Answer (a) proposes that the flows represent data internal to the system. Since the flows represent data produced by input devices or consumed by output devices, answer (a) is incorrect.

Answer (b) proposes that the flows are limited by the physical constraints of the devices. The main objective of transform analysis is to decompose a program into modules and identify their organization and communication. Therefore, the physical constraints of the devices are not considered during transform analysis and answer (b) is incorrect.

Answer (c) indicates that the system design should be independent of the format of the data. Since the I/O devices may require data formats that differ, answer (c) is correct.

Answer (d) proposes that system performance depends mainly on the time of the flows. However, the goal of transform analysis is to decompose a program into modules and identify their organization and communication. Performance is not considered during transform analysis and therefore answer (d) is incorrect.

Reference

1. Yourdon, E. and Constantine, L., *Structured Design: Fundamentals of a Discipline of Computer Program and Systems Design*, Prentice-Hall, 1986.

Question Which of the following statements are true about UML?

    I. UML provides software developers with a language for specifying and documenting the artifacts of software systems.

    II. UML represents a radical departure from the previous object-oriented development methods like Booch, OMT (Object Modeling Technique) and OOSE (Object-Oriented Software Engineering).

    III. UML is designed to be independent of the software development process.

    IV. An extensive knowledge of UML is enough for a software developer to succeed in an object-oriented software development project.

a) II, and IV
b) I and IV
c) II and III only
d) I and III only

Answer: d

Explanation

According to the Object Management Group (OMG), The Unified Modeling Language™(UML) is a standard language for specifying, visualizing, constructing, and documenting the way the world models not only application structure, behavior, and architecture, but also business processes and data structures.

The preface to the OMG's Unified Language Modeling Specification states that "UML defines a graphical language for visualizing, specifying, documenting, and constructing the artifacts of distributed object systems." This definition clearly encompasses the concept presented in option I that UML provides software developers with a language for specifying and documenting the artifacts of software systems. Therefore, option I is true.

Option II proposes that UML is a radical departure from the previous object-oriented development methods like Booch, OMT (Object Modeling Technique) and OOSE (Object-Oriented Software Engineering). However, the term "Unified" in The Unified Modeling Language refers to the unification of the work of Jim Rumbaugh, Grady Booch, and Ivar Jacobson, all of whom had proposed separate object-oriented modeling methods. Jim Rumbaugh is the chief developer of the Object Modeling Technique (OMT) and Ivar Jacobson is the inventor of the OOSE method. Therefore, option II is false, eliminating answers (a) and (c) as correct answers.

UML is a graphical notation used to express diagrams. This notation includes no discussion of the steps to be taken during design (i.e., process). Although the Unified Software Development Process is a process constructed to be used with UML, this process is entirely separate from UML. Therefore, option III is true.

Option IV proposes that an extensive knowledge of UML is sufficient for a software developer to succeed in an object-oriented software development project. However, an understanding of UML only provides an understanding of the design itself; it does not contain information on how to use the notation to develop a complete application from the design. UML alone does not contain sufficient information to guide the developer during the construction process. Therefore, option IV is false, eliminating answers (a) and (b) from being correct answers.

Answer (d) is the only answer that contained both correct options I and III.

References

1. OMG. *Unified Modeling Language Specification*. v1.5, March, 2001.

2. Fowler, M., and Scott, K., *UML Distilled: A Brief Guide to the Universal Modeling Language* 2nd ed., Addison-Wesley, 2000.

| 11 | III | SOFTWARE DESIGN |
| | C | Software design quality analysis and evaluation |

Question   Which of the following is NOT a factor to be considered when assessing design quality?

a)   Maintainability
b)   Reliability
c)   Stability
d)   Usability

Answer: c

Explanation

The assessment of design quality is based on the applicability of the software for its intended purpose. There are a variety of factors that may be used to assess design quality including functionality, reliability, usability, efficiency, maintainability, simplicity, and modularity. Design quality may be assessed using design reviews.

Maintainability is the ease with which changes may be made to a software system. These changes may be made to correct faults (corrective maintenance), improve performance or other attributes (perfective maintenance), or adapt to a changed environment (adaptive maintenance). A design should support the maintainability of the system by allowing these changes to be made with ease. Since maintenance is a factor to be considered when assessing design quality, answer (a) is incorrect.

Reliability refers to the ability of a system or component to perform its required functions under stated conditions for a specified period of time. Reliability includes the concept of predictability whereby the system behaves as expected over time. Since reliability is a factor to be considered when assessing design quality, answer (b) is incorrect.

Stability is not a design attribute. Software stability refers to the ease with which a software system can evolve while sustaining its design. Stability has an impact on the maintainability of the software system, but is not an attribute of the system design and cannot be known at design time. Therefore, stability is NOT a factor to be considered when assessing design quality and answer (c) is correct

Usability is the ease with which a user can learn to operate, prepare inputs for, and interpret outputs of a system or component. The usability of a system may be ascertained at design time through the use of design reviews of the user interface. Since usability is a factor to be considered when assessing design quality, answer (d) is incorrect.

References

1. Budgen, D., *Software Design*, Addison-Wesley, 1994.

2. Institute of Electrical and Electronics Engineers. *IEEE Standard Computer Dictionary: A Compilation of IEEE Std. Computer Glossaries*. IEEE New York, 1990.

Question   In structured design, a transaction center is

a) A module that controls the termination of tasks
b) A process of a data flow diagram that splits the process flow into different process paths
c) The set of data flows that appears between the afferent and efferent data flows
d) The high-level module that controls a set of low-level modules

Answer: b

Explanation

A transaction center is a DFD process that does not do actual transformation of the incoming data, rather, it serves to route the data to one or more processes. A transaction center is any DFD process that receives and analyses data, and depending on the results of this analysis, activates one or more processes. Usually, the transaction center activates a process chain instead of an isolated process, that is, it redirects the process flow into one of several available process paths. This usually appears in a DFD as a process containing a single incoming data flow and output data flows to two or more other processes. An application may contain multiple transaction centers.

Answer (a) proposes that a transaction center is a module that controls the termination of tasks. Since a transaction center is not a module, answer (a) is incorrect.

Answer (b) correctly defines a transaction center as a process of a data flow diagram that splits the process flow into different process paths. Answer (b) is the correct answer.

Answer (c) proposes that a transaction center is a set of data flows. A transaction center is a process that controls data flows rather being than one or more data flows itself. Therefore answer (c) is incorrect.

Answer (d) proposes that a transaction center is a module that controls a set of low level modules. Although a transaction center does indeed control data flows, a transaction center is a process, not a module. Therefore answer (d) is incorrect.

Reference

1. Yourdon, E. and Constantine, L., *Structured Design: Fundamentals of a Discipline of Computer Program and Systems Design*, Prentice-Hall, 1986.

Question What does coupling NOT depend on?

a) The references made from one component to another
b) The closeness of the operations in the functions
c) The degree of complexity in the interface between components
d) The amount of control one component has over the other

Answer: b

Explanation

Coupling is defined as the level of dependence between two or more components or modules. Coupling is also a measure of software design quality. Coupling is dependent on:

- The references from one component to another in which one component depends on another to complete its task
- The amount of data passed between components
- The control that one component has over another in which one component changes the state of another or tells another component to invoke a process
- The complexity of the interfaces between the component.

Answers (a), (c), and (d) are true characteristics of coupling. Answer (b) is describes cohesion, which refers to the degree to which a component's internal components are related. Therefore, answer (b) is the proper answer.

References

1. Pfleeger, S. L., *Software Engineering: Theory and Practice*, 2nd ed., Prentice-Hall, 2001.

2. Pressman, R., *Software Engineering: A Practitioner's Approach,* 6th ed., McGraw-Hill, 2005.

Question   Design is concerned with which of the following?

a) Identifying and describing the operational needs of the system
b) Performing a validation to see how well the system performs
c) Writing system requirements in a form that can be used for implementation
d) Describing how the system is to perform its tasks

Answer: d

Explanation

The design phase is the period of time in the software life cycle during which the designs for architecture, software components, interfaces, and data are created, documented, and verified to satisfy requirements.

The identification and description of the operational needs of the system is performed during the requirements engineering phase of software development. During requirements engineering, a complete description of the system to be developed is constructed including the functions of the software to be developed, the possible future extensions to the system, the documentation requirements, and the operational requirements of the system. Answer (a) is concerned with requirements, not design. Therefore, (a) is incorrect.

The validation of a system to see how well the system operates is performed during the verification and validation (testing) phase of software development. During verification and validation, the system is tested to see whether the software correctly implements its intended function as well as ensuring that the software implements the functionality contained in the requirements. Answer (b) is concerned with testing, not design. Therefore, (b) is incorrect.

Writing system requirements in a form that can be used as a basis for design and implementation is performed during the specification phase. During this phase, the requirements for a system or component are refined and expanded to the extent that they can form the basis for design. Answer (c) is concerned with specification, not design. Therefore, (c) is incorrect.

During the design phase, a model of the system is developed that describes how the system will perform its tasks to meet the users' requirements. This model is then decomposed into pieces (components or modules) that can be implemented. Answer (d) correctly states that design involves describing how the system is to perform its tasks.

Reference

1. Budgen, D., *Software Design,* 2nd ed., Addison-Wesley/Pearson, 2003.

Question   Which of the following is NOT a force that acts to encourage the generation of reference architectures?

a)   Future developers need to understand how to program future applications in a domain.

b)   A user community wants to interchange components and to interoperate among systems.

c)   Potential customers need a principled basis for comparison among systems.

d)   The key aspects of an application domain remain invariant over time.

Answer: d

Explanation

A software architecture represents a mapping of the functionality of a software system to software elements and data flows. It is a high-level system design that does not contain implementation details. Specifically, a software architecture consists of a high-level description of system components, definitions of relationships between components, and definitions of relationships between system components and external systems. A reference architecture is derived from a reference model and a software architecture pattern. It provides a high-level software architecture for a set of systems that share a domain. The reference architecture defines a common infrastructure used to construct these systems; it aids the designer in choosing an architecture for a specific application within the domain. The benefits of using reference architectures include providing guidance to developers when constructing new products, supplying an understanding of architectural components at a high level, and providing a common perspective to customers and users that can help them to compare design alternatives.

One purpose of a reference architecture is to provide a high-level understanding of system design for the applications developed based on the architecture. The ability of a reference architecture to provide guidance so that future developers understand how to program future applications in a domain is a primary motivation for the generation of a reference architecture. The guidance provided by a reference architecture can reduce development costs. Therefore, answer (a) is incorrect (since the question is asked in the negative).

Another primary benefit of a reference architecture is to provide understanding of the components of an architecture. This understanding allows users and developers to comprehend the implications of the architecture at a high level and also provides an understanding of the components that make up the architecture and the relationships between the components. A user community that desires to interchange components and to interoperate among systems requires such an understanding of the components, and therefore is a strong motivating force for the generation of reference architectures. Therefore, answer (b) is incorrect (since the question is asked in the negative).

Since a reference architecture provides an understanding of a set of systems developed for a domain by generalizing and abstracting components and their inter-relationships, the creation of a reference architecture provides potential customers with a common perspective and principled basis for comparison of systems. Therefore, answer (c) is incorrect (since the question is asked in the negative).

A reference architecture may be expected to change over time for some application domains. This flexibility is required for the architecture to continue to adequately represent the proper aspects of the applications developed for the domain as the domain changes and matures. Therefore, answer (d) is the correct answer.

Reference

1. Bass, L., Clements, P., and Kazman, R., *Software Architecture in Practice*, 2nd ed., Addison-Wesley, 2003.

16	III	SOFTWARE DESIGN
	D	Software design notations and documentation

Question The data flow diagram provides a mechanism for:

     I.   *Modeling system functions*

    II.   *Modeling databases*

   III.   *Modeling system information*

   IV.   *Modeling objects*

a) I and II
b) II and IV
c) I and III
d) II and IV

Answer: c

Explanation

Data flow diagrams (DFDs) are graphical representations of systems, showing data flows, data stores, data processes, and data sources/destinations. DFDs show logical storage of data as well as how data moves between processes. Since DFDs include data flows and data processes, DFDs allow the development of the information flow and functional aspects of a system at the same time. In addition, DFDs are hierarchical in nature, allowing the system to be represented at various levels of detail.

Option I indicates correctly that DFDs are used for functional modeling. DFD's may be partitioned into levels that represent increasing information flow and functional detail. Therefore, the DFD provides a mechanism for functional modeling as well as information flow modeling.

Option II incorrectly suggests that DFDs may be used for database modeling. DFDs provide a logical view of the data, not a physical view, and details of data formats and database representation are not included in DFDs. Therefore, answers (a), (b), and (d) are incorrect.

Option III correctly indicates that DFDs are used for modeling information flows within a system.

Option IV incorrectly suggests that DFDs may be used for object modeling. DFDs focus on the flow of information and the processes that operate on the information within a system. The organization of data is not considered. Therefore answers (b) and (d) are incorrect.

The only answer that contains both correct options I and III is answer (c).

Reference

1. Pressman, R., *Software Engineering: A Practitioner's Approach*, 6th ed., McGraw-Hill, 2005.

Question   Which of the following is least likely to be a benefit of a strict layered architecture?

     I.   *It facilitates extensibility.*

     II. *Implementation at each level is based solely on the interfaces of the layer below.*

     III. *It enhances system performance.*

a)   I only
b)   I and II only
c)   III only
d)   II and III only

Answer: c

Explanation

The layered architectural style organizes the software into layers, each of which provides a set of services. Each layer provides services to the layer above it (or outside it) and acts as a client to the services provided by the layer below it (or inside it). The layered architectural style allows designers to decompose a problem into ever increasing abstract steps; each layer is considered to be an increasing level of abstraction. In a strictly layered system, each layer is restricted to interacting only with its two adjacent layers.

Since layers are restricted to interacting with only their two adjacent layers, a layer is relatively easy to add or modify since such changes only affect the two adjacent layers. Option I correctly indicates that one of the benefits of a strict layered software architecture is extensibility. Therefore, answers (a) and (b) are incorrect as they identify option I as not being a benefit to the layered approach.

Option II correctly describes one characteristic of a strict layered architecture: the implementation at each level is based solely on the interfaces of the layer below. Therefore, answers (b) and (d) are incorrect as they identify option II as not being a benefit to the layered approach.

One of the disadvantages of the strict layered architectural style is that communication between nonadjacent layers must traverse any intermediate layers between the source and destination layers without skipping any layers. This requirement may result in performance degradation. Option III is the only option that identifies a characteristic that is not a benefit of the strictly layered architecture. Therefore, answer (c) is correct.

References

1. Bass, L., Clements, P., and Kazman, R., *Software Architecture in Practice*, 2nd ed., Addison-Wesley, 2003.

2. Pfleeger, S. L., *Software Engineering: Theory and Practice*, 2nd ed., Prentice-Hall, 2001.

Question Which of the following statements better describe the term "entity attribute"?

    I. An element (component) of a design that is structurally and functionally distinct from other elements and that is separately named and referenced.

    II. A subset of design entity attribute information that is specifically suited to the needs of a software project activity.

    III. A named characteristic, or property, of a design entity. It provides a statement of fact about the entity.

a) I only
b) II and III only
c) III only
d) I and II only

Answer: c

Explanation

IEEE Std 1016-1988, IEEE Recommended Practice for Software Design Descriptions defines a "design entity" (section 3.1) as "An element (component) of a design that is structurally and functionally distinct from other elements and that is separately named and referenced." Therefore, statement I above defines a design entity, not an entity attribute. Answers (a) and (d) include statement I and, therefore, are not accurate descriptions of the term "entity attribute."

IEEE Std 1016-1988, IEEE Recommended Practice for Software Design Descriptions defines a "design view" (section 3.2) as "A subset of design entity attribute information that is specifically suited to the needs of a software project activity." Therefore, statement II above defines a design view, not an entity attribute. Answers (b) and (d) include statement II and, therefore, are not accurate descriptions of the term "entity attribute."

IEEE Std 1016-1988, IEEE Recommended Practice for Software Design Descriptions defines an "entity attribute" (section 3.3) as "A named characteristic, or property, of a design entity. It provides a statement of fact about the entity." Therefore, statement III above defines an entity attribute. It follows logically that since the only answer that includes statement III and only statement III is answer (c), answer (c) is the correct answer.

Reference

1. IEEE Std 1016-1998, (Revision of IEEE Std 1016-1987), *IEEE Recommended Practice for Software Design Descriptions*, 1998.

Question   The following are all essential characteristics of an object EXCEPT:

a) Is a unit of instantiation
b) Has a unique identity
c) Is a unit of independent deployment
d) Encapsulates its state and behavior

Answer: c

Explanation

An object is defined as a run-time instance of a class or an instance of a class type created at execution time. It is a specific example of the general structure defined by a class. An object encapsulates both variables (state information) and methods (behavior) and is characterized by:

Identity: It acts as a single entity

State: It has properties that may change over the course of the object's lifetime

Behavior: It can take actions and have actions applied to it

Since an object is an instance of a class, objects are units of instantiation. Therefore, answer (a) correctly identifies an essential characteristic of an object.

Answer (b) correctly identifies a unique identity as an essential characteristic of an object.

Since an object must rely on other objects to provide additional behavior and to invoke behavior on itself in order to accomplish a task of any reasonable size, an object is not a unit of independent deployment. Therefore, answer (c) is correct.

Answer (d) correctly identifies the encapsulation of state and behavior as an essential characteristic of an object.

References

1. Meyer, B., *Object Oriented Software Construction*, 2nd ed., Prentice-Hall, 1997.

2. Budd, T., *An Introduction to Object-Oriented Programming*, 2nd ed., Addison-Wesley, 1997.

20	III	SOFTWARE DESIGN
	E	Software design strategies and methods

Question   Which of the following is NOT an attribute of a design pattern:

a)   Characterizes ways in which classes and objects distribute responsibility.

b)   Deals with the composition of classes or objects.

c)   Provides information regarding the pattern's appropriate use.

d)   Provides concrete classes for abstract classes.

Answer: d

Explanation

Christopher Alexander, the father of architectural design patterns, says "Each pattern describes a problem which occurs over and over again in our environment, and then describes the core of the solution to that problem, in such a way that you can use this solution a million times over, without ever doing it the same way twice." Software design patterns share this characteristic of providing a solution to a recurring problem within a context. A design pattern contains four components:

1. A name that describes the problem and the solution (briefly)

2. A description of when to apply the pattern

3. A description of the elements of the solution, their responsibilities, their relationships and collaborations

4. A description of the consequences of the application of the pattern, including benefits and drawbacks

Therefore, answer (a) is clearly included in the definition of a design pattern, specifically in the description of the elements of the solution that discusses the actions each element is responsible for, as well as the interconnections with other elements and their collaborations.

Answer (b) on the composition of classes or objects is also covered in the description of the elements of the solution. The discussion of the solution would include an explanation of how classes are composed of other classes and/or how objects are composed of other objects.

The information regarding the pattern's appropriate use, answer (c), is also covered in the four essential components of a design pattern. The use of a design pattern is included in the description of when to apply the pattern, which should encompass specific design problems, class and object structures that indicate an inflexible design, and a set of preconditions for applying the design pattern.

Answer (d) discusses an action that may be taken within a design pattern, but is not an attribute or characteristic of a design pattern. Therefore, answer (d) is the item that is not an attribute of a design pattern.

References

1. Gamma, E., Halm, R., Johnson, R. E., and Vlissides, J., *Design Patterns: Elements of Reusable Object-Oriented Software*, Addison Wesley, 1995.

2. Alexander, C., Ishikawa, S., Silverstein, M., Jacobson, M., Fiksdahl-King, I., and S. Angel, *A Pattern Language*, Oxford University Press, NY, 1977.

Question   A software system whose design is based on the principles of modularity and localization will result in modules that:

a)   Implement design patterns, with each design pattern only interacting locally with other design patterns

b)   Implement logically related processing elements that are relatively independent from other modules

c)   Have a minimum number of loops and conditional constructs and be relatively small in size

d)   Are designed using a top-down approach with processing implemented using a bottom-up approach

Answer: b

Explanation

Modularity is the principle that guides the decomposition of a system into a number of component modules. Modularity may also refer to the extent to which a system has been composed of separate parts. In a well-modularized system, each activity is performed by only one component and the inputs and outputs of all components are well defined (i.e., components have well-defined interfaces).

Localization is the principle that guides the decomposition process itself to cause highly related items to be placed in the same module, and items that are not highly related to be placed in different modules.

Modularity and localization are principles that underlie the concept of coupling (the degree of dependency that exists between modules) and cohesion (the degree to which a module's contents are related). A system that exhibits low coupling between its components and high cohesion within its components is easier to develop, test, and maintain. A system designed on the principles of modularity and localization will exhibit strong cohesion of internal components and loose coupling between modules.

Answer (a) suggests that the employment of the principles of modularity and localization will result in modules that contain design patterns in which each design pattern only interacts locally with other design patterns. The use of modularity and localization will not impact the interaction between design patterns significantly. Therefore, answer (a) is incorrect.

Answer (b) states that the employment of the principles of modularity and localization will result in a system containing modules that implement logically related processing elements that are relatively independent from other modules. This is another way of stating that the modules in the system will exhibit high cohesion and low coupling, characteristics that are a direct result of the use of modularity and localization. Therefore, answer (b) is correct.

Answer (c) indicates that the employment of the principles of modularity and localization will result in modules that have a minimum number of loops and conditional constructs and be relatively small in size. The quality of having a minimum number of loops and conditional constructs is a characteristic of the concept of "locality of reference", not of the use of modularity and localization in design. Therefore, answer (c) is incorrect.

Answer (d) indicates that a software system that is designed based on the principles of modularity and localization will result in modules that are designed using a top-down approach, with processing implemented using a bottom-up approach. However, the use of the principles of localization and modularization do not direct the development of modules. The use of localization and modularization is orthogonal to the module development process. Therefore, answer (d) is incorrect.

Reference

1. Booch, G., *Software Engineering with Ada*, 2nd ed., Benjamin/Cummings, 1987.

Question   Which of the following are the main components of a design method?

I.   *Representation: How to describe the design model*

II. *Process: What to do to produce the design model*

III. *Heuristics: How to adapt the model to specific types of problems*

a)   I only
b)   II only
c)   III only
d)   I, II, and III

Answer: d

Explanation

A design method is a set of guidelines, heuristics, procedures or steps to take in designing a system. This set of steps is arranged into an organized design process. A defined notation is used to express the results of a design process in a fashion understandable to developers. As part of the design process, the model is adapted to the specific problem to be solved by using heuristics. In addition, the examination of a design method's notation, process, and heuristics are also helpful in determining the limitations of a software design method. Since all three options listed in the question description are necessary components of a design method, answer (d) is the correct answer.

Reference

1. Budgen, D., *Software Design*, Addison-Wesley, 1994.

Question Which of the following characteristics are shared by object composition and implementation inheritance?

    I.   *Can be used at compile time to override operations*

    II. *Supports dynamic composition*

    III. *Supports code reuse*

    IV. *Separation of implementation from interface*

a)   I and III only

b)   II, III, and IV only

c)   III and IV only

d)   I, III, and IV only

Answer: c

Explanation

Object composition is defined as the assembling of an object from other objects to create more complex functionality. Since objects are runtime entities, this composition must happen dynamically at runtime as objects obtain references to other objects. In other words, an instance of one class possesses one or more attributes of another class.

Implementation inheritance is a form of inheritance in which a new implementation (child object) is defined in terms of one or more existing implementations (parent objects). Implementation inheritance allows the child object to reuse the parent objects' implementation as if it were its own. Inheritance results in simple and efficient access to features in the original (parent) object. In addition, child objects may reuse operations from the parents with their original implementations or with implementations specific to the child.

Option I proposes that both object composition and implementation inheritance can be used at compile-time to override operations. However, when using object composition, since objects are run-time entities, objects must be composed dynamically at runtime. Therefore, object composition cannot be used at compile time to override operations. The elimination of option I as a viable option eliminates answers (a) and (d) as correct answers.

Option II proposes that both object composition and implementation inheritance support dynamic composition. However, object implementations involved in implementation inheritance must be designated at compile time. Therefore, implementation inheritance cannot be used to support dynamic composition. The elimination of option II as a viable option eliminates answer (b) as a correct answer.

Option III proposes that both object composition and implementation inheritance support code reuse. One of the defining characteristics of inheritance, as well as one of its major benefits, is code reuse. Object composition also utilizes code reuse since one object uses another. Therefore, option III is true.

Option IV proposes that both object composition and implementation inheritance support the separation of implementation from interface. In object composition, the larger object being composed of other objects need only know the interface to the subservient objects, not the underlying implementation of such objects, preserving separation of implementation from interface. Similarly, in implementation inheritance, the child object need only know the interface of the parent object in order to use the parents' features, again preserving separation of implementation from interface. Therefore, option IV is true.

Since both options III and IV are true, the correct answer is (c).

References

1. Gamma, E., Halm, R., Johnson, R. E., and Vlissides, J., *Design Patterns: Elements of Reusable Object-Oriented Software*, Addison Wesley, 1995.

2. Meyer, B., *Object-Oriented Software Construction*, 2nd ed., Prentice-Hall, 1997.

Question During domain analysis, which of the following techniques should NOT be used to discover classes?

a) Identify each person, place, or thing involved with the system

b) Identify the operations that affect each object

c) Identify how objects relate to each other

d) Identify the packages in which each object will reside

Answer: d

Explanation

The set of applications used within a particular domain (e.g., banking) frequently share common characteristics. The identification of reusable portions of such applications could improve time to market and reduce development cost for future applications. Domain analysis is the process by which reusable components, concepts, and structures are identified, analyzed, and specified for an application domain. Domain analysis is carried out at a relatively high level of abstraction and focuses on supporting systematic and large-scale reuse. A variety of domain analysis methodologies exist, but the general steps include:

- Definition of the basic concepts (objects, categories, classes) of the domain, including boundary, scope, and vocabulary

- Identification of relationships and constraints among the concepts (objects) in the domain

- Discovery of the data that supports the concepts and the behavior provided by the concepts (objects)

Answer (a) indicates that each person, place, or thing involved with the system should be identified. This is clearly part of the step to identify the basic concepts of the domain. Therefore, answer (a) is incorrect, as it refers to a technique that should be used to discover classes.

Answer (b) indicates that the operations that affect each object in the system should be identified. The identification of operations is part of the step of discovering data and behavior provided by the objects in a domain. As operations are identified and associated with objects, new objects may be discovered. Therefore, answer (b) is incorrect, as it refers to a technique that should be used to discover classes.

Answer (c) indicates that the way in which objects relate to each other should be identified. This ascertaining of the relationships between objects is part of the domain analysis process. The identification of relationships may lead to the discovery of new objects. Therefore, answer (c) is incorrect, as it refers to a technique that should be used to discover classes.

Answer (d) indicates that the packages in which each object will reside should be identified. The allocation of objects to packages is an implementation issue and should not be performed during domain analysis or in any stage of requirements analysis. Therefore, answer (d) is the correct answer since the allocation of classes to packages is not part of domain analysis, nor can it be used to discover new classes.

References

1. Booch, G., *Software Engineering with Ada*, 2nd ed., Benjamin Cummings, 1987.

Question The model-view-controller architecture is useful for designing systems that have a graphical user interface because:

a) The appearance and behavior of the user interface can be modified without modifying the underlying data model,

b) Domain, entity and control objects have well-defined roles that help to reduce the system's complexity,

c) Graphical elements can be dynamically updated by using an event model,

d) Information storage can be controlled directly from graphical elements,

Answer: a

Explanation

The model-view-controller (MVC) architecture was developed to support user interfaces, specifically to separate the internal information in a system from the ways that the information can be presented. The main goal of the MVC architecture is to separate the domain (model) from the underlying control of the application from the user interface (view). The MVC architecture consists of three parts:

- Model represents the state of the system and is independent of the visual representation
- View representation that the user sees; can vary across platforms
- Controller directs how system interacts with events such as mouse clicks

One of the main advantages to the MVC architecture is support of multiple different user representations of the same information. The system can display the model to the user in a variety of appearances and behaviors without impacting the underlying data model. Other advantages include more modular design, increased reuse, and ease of extensibility.

Answer (a) correctly indicates that a significant advantage to using the MVC architecture when designing systems that have a graphical user interface is that the appearance and behavior of the user interface can be modified without modifying the underlying data model. Therefore, answer (a) is correct.

Although the MVC architecture is usually implemented with distinct domain, entity, and control objects, the advantages of such implementation cannot be directly attributed to the use of the MVC architecture. Therefore answer (b) is incorrect.

Answer (c) states that graphical elements can be dynamically updated by using an event model. Although this statement is true, it is merely a description of how the MVC architecture works and does not address the usefulness of the MVC architecture. Therefore, answer (c) is incorrect.

Answer (d) proposes that information storage can be controlled directly from graphical elements. However, one main precept of the MVC architecture is the separation of graphical elements from the control elements. Therefore, allowing graphical elements to control information storage is an undesirable violation of the MVC architecture. Answer (d) is incorrect.

Reference

1. Constantine, L. L., and Lockwood, L. A. D., *Software for Use: A Practical Guide to the Essential Models and Methods of Usage-Centered Design*, Addison-Wesley, 1999.

Question A collection of systems, constructed from a common set of software assets, that shares a managed set of features is known as:

a) A software product line
b) A product portfolio
c) A strategic architecture
d) An enterprise management system

Answer: a

Explanation

A software product line is defined as a set of software-intensive systems that share a common, managed set of features satisfying the specific needs of a particular market segment or mission and that are developed from a common set of core assets in a prescribed way. An individual product is constructed by taking the appropriate components from a set of common assets and tailoring them to meet a specific need. Therefore, answer (a) clearly meets the definition provided and is the correct answer.

A product portfolio is defined as a set of different products that a company produces. The range of products offered by a company is ideally balanced, containing some mature products, others in development, and others on the verge of being introduced into the market. A product portfolio typically contains applications with a much wider range of functionality than a product line. In addition, a product portfolio is not necessarily constructed using a common set of software assets. Therefore, answer (b) is incorrect.

A strategic architecture is an architecture that is shared by the products in a software product line. The strategic architecture allows the products to be explicitly tailored to different needs while supporting reuse of assets by providing a common, shared infrastructure. The strategic architecture provides a unifying vision for products as they evolve. Although the assets may embody the principles of a strategic architecture, they are not synonymous with that architecture. Therefore, answer (c) is incorrect.

An enterprise management system is a set of tools that enable management of the technical infrastructure of a company, including data storage and retrieval. Although an enterprise management system may be composed of a distributed set of network and element management systems, these systems may not be based on a common set of software assets (nor need they share a common set of features). Therefore, answer (d) is incorrect.

Reference

1. Bass, L., Clements, P., and Kazman, R., *Software Architecture in Practice*, 2nd ed., Addison-Wesley, 2003.

Question A high quality-design for a software module will exhibit which of the following attributes?

    I.   The set of tasks within the module are logically related.

    II. Coupling of the module with other modules is low.

    III. The module is simple to test.

a)   I, II, and III only
b)   I and II only
c)   I only
d)   I and III only

Answer: a

Explanation

The design quality of a module is highly dependent on the degree of cohesion within the module and the degree of coupling between the module and other modules in the system. Cohesion refers to the degree to which a module's internal components are related. Cohesion implies that a module encapsulates only the data and operations that are closely related to one another and to the module itself. Coupling is defined as the level of dependence between two or more components or modules. Coupling is dependent on the references from one module to another, the amount of data passed between modules, the control that one module has over another, and the complexity of the interfaces between the module and others. In addition, the goal of module design is to have each module be responsible for a single, clearly identifiable portion of functionality. Therefore, the module should be simple to test.

Option I contains a definition of cohesion, a desirable characteristic of a module.

Option II describes the ideal state of a module with respect to coupling.

Option III describes the ideal state of a module with respect to testing.

Since all options describe attributes of a high-quality design for a software module, the correct answer is (a).

Reference

1. Pressman, R., *Software Engineering: A Practitioner's Approach*, 6th ed., McGraw-Hill, 2005.

The SoundAll Company has an idea for a new commercial application, Not-Napster, an audio Web site that allows users to purchase CDs and cassette tapes online. Not-Napster allows users to sample music from any CD or tape in stock before ordering. Users can download audio clips that contain no more than 20% of a musical selection, but not the entire selection. The main page displays a welcome message, current specials, and new releases, and the customer's contact information, including e-mail address, phone number, and mailing address. The main page allows the user to select a music category and display all available selections. The main page also allows the user to search for items based on topic, song title, songwriter, artist, and so on. Each selection displayed contains a link to at least one audio clip from the selection. Two engineers have been given the responsibility for developing the architectural design for the Not-Napster system.

Question Of the following architectural styles, which would be more suitable to use as the basis for engineering Not-Napster?

a) Layered
b) Process control
c) Hierarchical
d) Pipe-and-filter

Answer: a

Explanation

The layered architectural style views a system as a series of concentric circles in which each circle provides services to its outer circle and calls on services on its inner layer. Protocols define how each pair of layers interact. The layered architectural style is used when the system can easily be defined in terms of layers of abstraction where each layer provides functionality required to the next layer. The Not-Napster application is a typical multi-tier application in which the interface, business logic, and database are clear layers of functionality. Therefore, answer (a) is correct.

The process control architectural style is intended for use in systems whose main responsibility is to maintain specified properties of process outputs at or near specified reference values. The components used in a process control architecture typically include a controller, a sensor, a monitor, a process and a feedback or feedforward loop. A typical example of a process control system is a temperature-control system. The Not-Napster system does not require feedback and adjustment in order to fulfill its functionality. Therefore, answer (b) is incorrect.

The hierarchical architectural style is a form of a call-and-return architectural style in which a system is viewed as a hierarchy of procedures. The top-level procedure acts as the main program, calling other procedures in the proper order to accomplish the system's tasks. The hierarchical architectural style uses a single thread of execution, in which one module passes control to another and awaits its completion. Upon completion of the called module, control is then returned to the calling module. One main drawback to this architectural style is it does not easily support event-driven systems. Since the Not-Napster application is highly user-driven and, therefore, event-driven, the hierarchical architectural style is not a good fit for supporting the Not-Napster application. Therefore, answer (c) is incorrect.

The pipe-and-filter architectural style is used in systems that involve a series of independent transformations on ordered data, usually taking place in a sequential fashion. The pipe-and-filter architectural style views a system as a series of data flows called pipes, and a series of transformations called filters. The system is viewed as a composition of filters, with data flowing between the filters. Systems that have a pipe-and-filter architecture lend themselves to batch processing. In addition, due to their data flow orientation, systems that have a pipe-and-filter architecture do not easily support user interaction. Since the Not-Napster system is highly user interactive and contains no batch processing, a pipe-and-filter architecture is not a good selection to support this application. Therefore, answer (d) is incorrect.

References

1. Pressman, R., *Software Engineering: A Practitioner's Approach*, (6th ed.), McGraw-Hill, 2004.

2. Shaw, M. and Garlan, D., *Software Architecture, Perspectives on an Emerging Discipline*, Prentice-Hall, 1996.

3. Bass, L., Clements, P., and Kazman, R., *Software Architecture in Practice*, 2nd ed., Addison-Wesley, 2003.

138

A design team is working on the design of a payroll system. The system is being revised to accommodate new features that the customer desires. Previous versions of the design were not well documented, and the team is taking advantage of the current version to document the new design.

Question Analysis of the previous design noted that functions were grouped into modules in a haphazard way. This design property is BEST described as:

a) Coincidental cohesion
b) Logical cohesion
c) Content coupling
d) Common coupling

Answer: a

Explanation

Coupling is defined as the level of dependency that exists between modules. Decomposition should be done in such a way that the modules are as independent as possible from one another.

Cohesion is defined as the degree to which a module's instructions are related. Decomposition should be done in such a way that a module's contents are as highly related as possible.

Coincidental cohesion is defined as modules whose contents are unrelated. The instructions in these modules have little or no relationship to one another and were put into the module for reasons of convenience. Coincidental cohesion is the worst form of cohesion as it results in systems that are difficult to maintain and extend. Haphazard grouping of functions into modules is characteristic of coincidental cohesion. Therefore, answer (a) is correct.

Logical cohesion exists when functions of a similar type are grouped in the same module. These instructions appear to be related, as they fall into the same logical class of functions. Since logical cohesion suggests that there is an organization to the way that functions are grouped into modules; this grouping is not haphazard. Therefore, answer (b) is incorrect.

Content coupling exists when a module changes the data of another module. However, since coupling refers to the degree to which modules are dependent upon one another, not to the way in which functions are grouped into modules, answer (c) is incorrect.

Common coupling exists when modules share data. Common coupling frequently occurs in modules that refer to the same global data area. However, since coupling refers to the degree to which modules are dependent upon one another, not to the way in which functions are grouped into modules, answer (d) is incorrect.

References

1. Van Vliet, H., *Software Engineering: Principles and Practice*, 2nd ed., Wiley and Sons, New York, NY, 2000.

2. Pfleeger, S. L., *Software Engineering: Theory and Practice*, 2nd ed., Prentice-Hall, 2001.

A design team is working on the design of a payroll system. The system is being revised to accommodate new features that the customer desires. Previous versions of the design were not well documented, and the team is taking advantage of the current version to document the new design.

Question   The BEST argument for improving coupling across the design, from highly coupled to loosely coupled, is to:

a) Enable the design review to proceed faster and allow more time for coding and testing

b) Increase the ease of scheduling and the delegation of implementation

c) Create a system that is easier to test and maintain

d) Create a system whose user interface will be distributed across various objects

Answer: c

Explanation

Answer (a) asserts that better coupling within the design would enable the design review to proceed faster and allow more time for coding and testing. However, the design review time is not correlated to the amount of coupling in the design. The quality of the design as a whole, as well as the preparation of the participants, affects the time needed to review the design. Therefore, answer (a) is incorrect.

The ease of scheduling and delegation of implementation, despite the assertion of answer (b), are only moderately affected by the degree of coupling in the design. Although it makes sense to delegate a set of dependent modules to the same implementation team, If the entire system is composed of interdependent modules, identifying groups of modules to delegate to different teams may be somewhat more difficult. However, this difficulty has a very minimal impact on the overall development of the application. Therefore, answer (b) is incorrect.

The largest and longest-ranging impact of poor coupling in a software design and the resulting product is on testing and maintenance. Poor coupling results in modules that are highly dependent on other modules. Since maintenance involves changing a module, any change to a module has the potential to impact all of the modules with which that module is interdependent, making maintenance difficult. In addition, the high degree of module interdependence that results from poor coupling means that testing cannot be easily isolated to a single module. The greater the degree of dependency between modules, the greater the degree of complexity in testing such modules, as all dependencies must be tested. Therefore, answer (c) is correct.

The benefit of creating a system whose user interface will be distributed across various objects is unclear. In addition, the restructuring of the system to decrease coupling among modules may or may not impact the distribution of the user interface across objects. Therefore, answer (d) is incorrect.

Reference

1. Van Vliet, H., *Software Engineering: Principles and Practice*, 2nd ed., Wiley and Sons, New York, NY, 2000.

Area editor: Susan K. Land

IV. *Software Construction*

A)	Construction planning
B)	Code design
C)	Data design and management
D)	Error processing
E)	Source code organization
F)	Code documentation
G)	Construction quality assurance
H)	System integration and deployment
I)	Code tuning
J)	Construction tools

Question Two different implementations of a fully tested abstract class (or interface) have been created. If members of the software engineering team are to be able to correctly select the appropriate implementation to use, then the documentation for each of these implementations must include:

     I.   *A list of functions available and calling conventions*

     II.   *The source code for the implementation*

     III.   *Information about the side effects and resource usage for each function*

     IV.   *Names of the authors of each implementation and change history*

a) I and II only
b) I and III only
c) I, II, and III only
d) I, II, III, and IV

Answer: b

Explanation

The purpose of an abstract class (or interface) is only to support the modeling of shared attributes and operations. Since this generalization is never instantiated, its use requires an implementation. In order to provide software engineers with enough information to select an implementation from multiple choices, implementation specifications should provide a list of the functions with the associated calling conventions as well as information about any side effects or resource usage.

References

1. Troelsen, A., *COM and .NET Interoperability*, Apress, 2002.

2. Bruegge, B., and A.H. Dutoit, *Object-Oriented Software Engineering*, Prentice-Hall, 2000.

A new engineer has been assigned to a project team. The current project is 1 month into construction, and another 6 months of construction are expected. The engineer discovers that the only design document is an overview of the logical architecture. There are over 70 source code files, most over 600 lines long, residing in a single folder.

Question   It is very difficult to follow the module design of the system, but there appears to be redundant functionality in many of the source code files. The best steps for improvement would be to:

I.   *Combine files together to reduce the number of files*

II.   *Rework files to group functionality together*

III. *Use folders to group related files together*

IV.   *Change programming languages*

a)   I and II only
b)   I and III only
c)   II and III only
d)   II and IV only

Answer: c

Explanation

The correct answer, c, describes the ideal solution. The project has just begun construction and has produced a low-quality set of source files (poor cohesion and coupling, no physical folder structure, files too long). Items II and II address these problems. Item I describes combining files to reduce the total number. This will only add to the existing problem because it will probably increase coupling and decrease cohesion. Item IV proposes changing programming languages. The problem described is a result of the programming process and is independent of programming language or implementation method.

Reference

1. McConnell, S., *Code Complete*, 2nd ed., Microsoft Press, 2004.

Question   Which of the following is NOT required of a software component?

a)   Must be a unit of independent deployment
b)   Must support reuse
c)   Must be encapsulated
d)   Must expose source code for modification

Answer: d

Explanation

The idea that software should be componentized - built from prefabricated *components* — was first described by Douglas McIlroy in 1968. The modern concept of a software component was largely defined by Brad Cox, who set out to create an infrastructure and market for these components by inventing the Objective C programming language. Microsoft pioneered the actual deployment of component software with its Object Linking and Embedding (OLE) and Component Object Model (COM). Both of these ideas are based on the encapsulation and simplification of object interfaces.

The meaning of software component has changed over time. It can best be described loosely as a software technology for encapsulating software functionality. Clemens Szyperski and David Messerschmitt give the following five criteria that characterize a software component:

- Multiple-use
- Non-context-specific
- Composable with other components
- Encapsulated (i.e., non-investigable through its interfaces)
- A unit of independent deployment and versioning

References

1. Proceedings, NATO Conference on Software Engineering, *Mass Produced Software Components*, Germany, 1968.

2. Cox, B. and A. Novobilski,, *Object-Oriented Programming: An Evolutionary Approach*, 2nd ed., Addison-Wesley, 1991.

3. Messerschmitt, D., and Szyperski, C., *Software Ecosystem: Understanding an Indispensable Technology and Industry*, MIT Press, 2003.

Question   The most important characteristic of an abstract data type is:

a)   The fact that knowledge about the implementation of an abstract data type can be used for memory optimization

b)   The fact that all signatures are encapsulated within the abstract data type's interfaces

c)   The separation of the implementation of the abstract data type from its use

d)   The polymorphism that results from defining a data structure as an abstract data type

Answer: c

Explanation

The IEEE Standard Glossary of Software Engineering Terminology defines an abstract data type as: "a data type for which only the properties of the data and the operations to be performed on the data are specified, without concern for how the data will be represented or how the operations will be implemented." An abstract data type is represented by an interface that hides the representation of the data and the implementation of the operations. Users of an abstract data type remain focused on the the interface, rather than the implementation.

The most frequently occurring abstract data types include:

- String
- List
- Stack
- Queue
- Binary search tree
- Priority queue

References

1. IEEE Std 610.12, *IEEE Standard Glossary of Software Engineering Terminology*, IEEE Press, 2002.

2. Goodrich, M. T., R. Tamassia, and D. Mount, *Data Structures and Algorithms in C++*, Wiley, 2004

Question An engineer is tasked to verify a software release for a mission-critical system. The plan is for the release of software for verification to occur on a Monday, with verification complete the following Friday. The release turns out not to be available until Thursday. The best route for the engineer is to:

a) Verify release criteria regardless of time line

b) Do whatever testing can be done by Friday

c) Volunteer to work over the weekend

d) Relax release criteria

152

Answer: a

Explanation

Since the question clearly specifies that the engineer's job is to verify a mission-critical application, the best route for the engineer is to stick to his or her responsibility of verifying the system. Although it may be necessary to work additional hours or to relax the release criteria, these actions do not guarantee the completion of system verification.

Reference

1. McConnell, S., *Software Project Survival Guide*, Microsoft Press, 1997.

Question Partitioning systems into the smallest components, while maximizing reuse, will diminish which of the following:

    I.   *Efficiency*

    II.   *Robustness in the face of evolution*

    III. *Manageability of the variety of configurations*

a)   I only
b)   I and II only
c)   II and III only
d)   I, II, and III

Answer: a

Explanation

Partitioning an application requires the division of source code into separate application components based on the type of work that each portion of code performs. A partitioned application is one that contains two or more components. A typical example of partitioning occurs when there is a primary component, *application.exe*, supported by any number of code libraries, or DLLs. Partitioning can make development, deployment, and maintenance of an application easier and more flexible if applied appropriately. However, there is an increased cost associated with the requirement to support cross-component communication. If partitioning is applied with too much rigor, it can lead to a significant decrease in efficiency.

References

1. Campbell, S., Swigart, S., Carver, B. et al., *101 Microsoft Visual Basic .NET Applications*, Microsoft Press, 2003.

2. Szyperski, C., *Component Software*, ACM Press, 1998.

A design team is working on the design of a payroll system. The system is being revised to accommodate new features that the customer desires. Previous versions of the design were not well documented, and the team is taking advantage of the current version to document the new design.

Question   During product implementation, a mixture of experienced and inexperienced developers were assigned to the project. The developers are not using consistent processes, and expectations have not been clearly defined. During code inspection, the lead developer told the inexperienced developers that their code was difficult to follow and understand. Inspecting their work would need to be rescheduled to give them an opportunity to improve their code. As far as this software organization is concerned, which is the MOST effective way to improve the understandability of their code?

a)   The developers need to improve the naming of variables and functions.

b)   The developers need to follow well-known industry coding standards in their work.

c)   The developers need to follow company coding standards in their work.

d)   The developers need to explain their work to their teammates so that they can better understand it.

Answer: c

Explanation

Option (c) is the correct choice because following existing company-specific coding standards will provide the most effective way to improve the comprehension of developed code within the company.

Option (a) is not correct because improving the names of variables and methods only addresses a portion of the readability problem. Option (b) would be a rational choice. However, the organization's coding standards need to be followed, and the internal standard may differ from a preexisting industry standard. Option (d) is incorrect, because explaining one's own work only works for a short period of time at best.

Reference

1. Pfleeger, S.L., Software Engineering Theory and Practice, 2nd ed., Prentice-Hall, 2001.

V. Software Testing

A)	Types of tests
B)	Test levels
C)	Testing strategies
D)	Test design
E)	Test coverage of code
F)	Test coverage of specifications
G)	Test execution
H)	Test documentation
I)	Test management

A procedure computes the average of 5 or fewer numbers that lie between two bounding values. It also computes the sum and the total number of values used to compute the average. The procedure's PDL implementation is:

```
PROCEDURE average

INTERFACE RETURNS average, total.input, total.valid;
INTERFACE ACCEPTS value, minimum, maximum;

TYPE value[1:100] IS SCALAR ARRAY;
TYPE average, total.input, total.valid;
     minimum, maximum, sum IS SCALAR;
TYPE i IS INTEGER;

(L01) i = 1;
(L02) total.input = total.valid = 0;
(L03) sum = 0;
(L04) DO WHILE value[i] <> -999 AND total.input < 5
(L05)    increment total.input by 1;
(L06)    IF value[i] >= minimum AND value[i] <= maximum
(L07)       THEN increment total.valid by 1;
(L08)            sum = sum + value[i]
(L09)       ELSE skip
(L10)    ENDIF
(L11)    increment i by 1;
(L12) ENDDO
(L13) IF total.valid > 0
(L14)    THEN average = sum / total.valid;
(L15)    ELSE average = -999;
(L16) ENDIF
(L17) END average
```

Question How many simple (i.e., not counting loops) definition–use chains (simple D–U chains) does variable "sum" have?

a) 0

b) 2

c) 3

d) 4

Answer: c

Explanation

Definition–use (D–U) chains can be used during data flow analysis, to help design and construct a set of well-organized, white-box test cases.

The variable "sum" is defined at L03, defined and used at L08, and used at L14. Hence, the three use definition–use chains are L03–L08, L08–L14, and L03–L14 (L08–L08 is not considered a D–U chain).

References

1. Jorgensen, P.C., *Software Testing: A Craftsman's Approach*, CRC Press, 2002.

2. Pressman, R., *Software Engineering: A Practitioner's Approach*, McGraw-Hill, 2005.

3. Sommerville, I., *Software Engineering*, Addison-Wesley, 2004.

4. van Vliet, H. *Software Engineering: Principles and Practice*, John Wiley & Sons, 2000.

A procedure computes the average of 5 or fewer numbers that lie between two bounding values. It also computes the sum and the total number of values used to compute the average. The procedure's PDL implementation is:

```
PROCEDURE average
INTERFACE RETURNS average, total.input, total.valid;
INTERFACE ACCEPTS value, minimum, maximum;

TYPE value[1:100] IS SCALAR ARRAY;
TYPE average, total.input, total.valid;
     minimum, maximum, sum IS SCALAR;
TYPE i IS INTEGER;

(L01) i = 1;
(L02) total.input = total.valid = 0;
(L03) sum = 0;
(L04) DO WHILE value[i] <> -999 AND total.input < 5
(L05)     increment total.input by 1;
(L06)     IF value[i] >= minimum AND value[i] <= maximum
(L07)         THEN increment total.valid by 1;
(L08)             sum = sum + value[i]
(L09)         ELSE skip
(L10)     ENDIF
(L11)     increment i by 1;
(L12) ENDDO
(L13) IF total.valid > 0
(L14)     THEN average = sum / total.valid;
(L15)     ELSE average = -999;
(L16) ENDIF
(L17) END average
```

Question What is the cyclomatic complexity of this piece of code?

a)   5

b)   6

c)   13

d)   4

Answer: b

Explanation

Cyclomatic complexity (also known as McCabe's complexity metric) can be computed by representing the code as a directed flow graph, and counting the number of regions in the graph. Alternatively, the formula $E - N + 2$ can be used (where E is the number of edges in the graph, and N the number of nodes). A third method for calculating cyclomatic complexity is to add one to the number of predicate nodes in the graph (predicate nodes correspond to a logical branch, i.e., a loop or conditional statement). This third method is the easiest to use when no flow graph already exists; assuming a program has no *goto* statements, its cyclomatic complexity is one more than the number of simple conditional statements contained in the logic.

Using this method, there are three lines of PDL with conditions (L04, L06, and L13). However, where Boolean operators are used in a condition, each simple condition must be counted individually. Since L04 and L06 each use the "and" operator, there are five conditions in the code (two in L04, two in L06, and one in L13). This yields a cyclomatic complexity of 6.

References

1. Pressman, R., *Software Engineering: A Practitioner's Approach*, McGraw-Hill, 2005.

2. Sommerville, I., *Software Engineering*, Addison-Wesley, 2004.

An engineer is testing a system and gathers the following data:

Module	Lines of Code	Defects
X	5,000	320
Y	10,000	700
Z	5,000	730

Question The system is scheduled for release in one week. With limited time available, where would the testing effort be best applied?

a) X and Y only
b) Z only
c) Y only
d) X, Y, and Z

Answer: b

Explanation

The testing effort should concentrate on the code with the highest defect density, because code with a higher defect density is more likely to negatively affect the system's behavior. The defect density for a module is defined to be the percentage of defects found in the module per lines of code. The defect densities for modules X, Y, and Z are:

Module	Lines of Code	Defects	Defect Density
X	5,000	320	6.4%
Y	10,000	700	7.0%
Z	5,000	730	14.6%

One could argue that answer (d) is viable, because, although Module Z should receive most of the attention, it should not necessarily be tested exclusively. However, in the absence of additional information, answer (d) implies that the three modules will be tested evenly, which would not be a wise testing strategy, given the markedly high defect rate already found in the module. Hence, answer (b) is the better answer.

This problem also assumes that the discovered defect rate variations are due to differences in software quality, not because Modules X and Y were tested less aggressively. We assume that the modules were tested with similar coverage and rigor, so that their defect rates can be legitimately compared.

References

1. McConnell, S., *Code Complete*, Microsoft Press, 2004.

2. Pfleeger, S.L., Hatton, L., and Howell, C.H., *Solid Software*, Prentice-Hall, 2002.

Question The primary objective of test case design is to derive a set of tests that

a) Are most likely to be successful
b) Have a high probability of failure
c) Are most likely to uncover defects in software
d) Support tracking

Answer: c

Explanation

The goal of software testing has evolved as software engineering has matured. This maturation has resulted in an increasingly aggressive testing mindset. We can presume that complex software contains defects, especially at the outset of testing. The tester's job is to find these defects, and test cases should be developed that maximize the probability of uncovering them. The notion that "successful" tests (i.e., tests that do not reveal a software defect) are most useful is both outdated and counterproductive.

Although documenting test results is important, tracking is certainly not the primary consideration during test case design.

References

1. Beizer, B., *Software Testing Techniques*, Van Nostrand Reinhold, 1990.

2. Metzger, R.C., *Debugging by Thinking*, Elsevier Digital Press, 2004.

3. Pressman, R., *Software Engineering: A Practitioner's Approach*, McGraw-Hill, 2005.

Question Equivalence partitioning is

a) A modular programming technique in which the application domain is subdivided into similarly sized functional areas

b) A black box testing technique that divides the input domain of a program into classes of data from which test cases can be derived

c) An object-oriented design technique for improving program structure by replacing inheritance with delegation

d) A software project management technique for distributing test responsibility within a project

Answer: b

Explanation

Possible inputs to a computer program can be categorized into disjoint sets of input data called equivalence classes. These classes are deliberately defined such that if a defect is found (or not found) for one test case in the class, the error is likely to be found (or not found) for all of the other test cases in the class. This testing strategy is designed to help address the goal of maximizing testing coverage while minimizing the number of test cases required for doing so.

Answer (a) describes decomposition, whereas answer (c) describes a refactoring technique. Answer (d) alludes to the maxim that testing responsibility ought to be organizationally separated from development responsibility. These other possible answers are valid concepts, but they do not describe equivalence partitioning. Therefore, the correct answer is (b).

References

1. Ould, M.A., and Unwin, C., *Testing in Software Development*, Cambridge University Press, 1986.

2. Pfleeger, S.L., Hatton, L., and Howell, C.H., *Solid Software*, Prentice-Hall, 2002.

3. Pressman, R., *Software Engineering: A Practitioner's Approach*, McGraw-Hill, 2005.

Question Which of the following should be included in a unit test plan?

      I.   *A source of test data and expected results*

     II.   *List of expected failures*

    III.   *List of features to be tested*

    IV.   *Characteristics of the input and output of the unit to be tested*

a)   I and III only

b)   I, II, and IV only

c)   I, III, and IV only

d)   I, II, III, and IV

Answer: c

Explanation

Unit test plans should contain pretest information, such as brief descriptions of the software and features to be tested, input/output descriptions, initial conditions assumed, and expected results of the test. They should also contain resultant information, such as the date the test was run, and the test results.

Software failures can be documented and categorized, but it is not correct to say that "expected failures" are part of the unit test plans. Expected output and actual output should be included (with differences between the two indicating a software failure), but this does not constitute documenting "expected failures" in the test plan.

References

1. Beizer, B., *Software System Testing and Quality Assurance*, Van Nostrand Reinhold, 1984.

2. Jorgensen, P.C., *Software Testing: A Craftsman's Approach*, CRC Press, 2002.

3. Schmauch, C.H., *ISO 9000 for Software Developers*, ASQC Quality Press, 1994.

Question Which of the following do NOT affect the accuracy of the reliability estimate during statistical testing?

      I.   *The validity of the usage profile*

     II.   *The number of test cases executed*

    III.   *The programming language used to implement the code*

    IV.   *The cyclomatic complexity of the code*

a)   I and II only

b)   II and III only

c)   III and IV only

d)   I and III only

Answer: c

Explanation

The goal of reliability testing (or statistical testing) is to demonstrate that a system meets its specified reliability requirements. To accomplish this, a usage profile (or operational profile) needs to be developed. This profile should reflect the normal use of the system. Test data and test cases are then generated to use with the operational profile. Failures are tallied as these tests are executed, allowing system reliability to be quantified, assuming that a statistically sufficient number of tests are run.

The accuracy of the resulting reliability estimate depends upon the two inputs into the testing process: the usage profile and the test cases. Factors such as programming language and cyclomatic complexity may affect product reliability, but they do not affect the accuracy of the reliability estimate.

References

1. Dyer, M., *The Cleanroom Approach to Quality Software Development*, John Wiley & Sons, 1992.

2. Sommerville, I., *Software Engineering*, Addison-Wesley, 2004.

Question The use of capture replay tools for graphical user interface testing suffers from which of the following problems:

    I.   *The execution of the test cases cannot be automated.*

    II. *Test cases may break if widgets are moved in the interface.*

    III. *Good test cases must be created and recorded manually.*

    IV. *The test cases cannot be reused if the implementation of the application is changed while leaving the interface unchanged.*

a)   I and III only
b)   I, II, and III only
c)   II and III only
d)   III and IV only

Answer: c

Explanation

Capture replay tools record keystrokes, cursor positions, and mouse clicks, allowing a test to be automated and rerun without direct user interaction. This eliminates answers (a) and (b), because capture replay tools enable automation. It is true that the test cases must be created and recorded manually, and this is often a time-consuming process. Choosing between answers (c) and (d) depends upon whether such test cases are more likely to break if the interface changes [in which case answer (c) is correct] or if the implementation changes [meaning answer (d) is correct].

If the user interfaces change (i.e., the position of buttons or checkboxes, the fields listed in menu bars, the order of submenu listings, etc.), the test cases may need to be rerecorded with the updated interface. However, implementation changes not affecting the user interface will not normally affect test cases constructed with a capture replay tool. Hence, answer (c) is the best answer.

Reference

1. Kaner, C., Falk, J., and Nguyen, H.Q., *Testing Computer Software*, John Wiley & Sons, 1999.

Question Structural tests derived from the implementation will NOT help the tester detect the following problems:

    I.   *Performance problems with the code*

    II. *Errors of omitted requirements*

    III. *Problems arising from very large and very small numbers*

    IV. *References through NULL pointers*

a)   I and II only
b)   II and III only
c)   I, III, and IV only
d)   I, II, III, and IV

Answer: a

Explanation

Structural testing (also known as white-box or glass-box testing) involves test cases generated directly from the source code (as opposed to functional or black-box testing, which is based primarily on requirement specifications). Structural tests, with their strong links to the source code, are especially suitable for detecting errors such as bad pointer references, as well as large or small number problems.

On the other hand, structural testing is much less likely to discover unimplemented requirements, because structural tests, by definition, examine code that has been implemented, not code that has been omitted. (Functional tests are more likely to reveal unmet requirements.) Similarly, performance problems are more likely to be discovered when the entire system is being tested, and most structural testing occurs at the unit level. Therefore, structural tests are unlikely to uncover performance problems. Hence, answer (a) is the best answer.

References

1. Jorgensen, P.C., *Software Testing: A Craftsman's Approach*, CRC Press, 2002.

2. Sommerville, I., *Software Engineering*, Addison-Wesley, 2004.

3. Whittaker, J.W., *How to Break Software: A Practical Guide to Testing*, Addison-Wesley, 2002.

A company is developing an inventory-tracking application. Their testing has been primarily black box — functional testing. The rationale is that this is not a mission-critical application, in which safety or severe financial loss is considered to be a potential risk. The company has now learned that one of their customers is using the application to manage and track inventories of controlled substances.

Question   The software development company should:

a) Conduct a risk analysis to verify that their current test strategy is effective at uncovering potential defects that could put the customer at risk of mismanaging their inventory.

b) Not change their test strategy since they expect that the software will continue to work well for their customers under these circumstances.

c) Definitely include white-box testing into their current test plan. They should regression test all of their code to verify its correctness.

d) Management should review and revise their testing policy.

Answer: a

Explanation

Answers (b), (c), and (d) may all be legitimate courses of action, but it is impossible to determine their appropriateness without first conducting a risk analysis. More specifically, answers (b) and (c) are mutually exclusive; either the current strategy is sufficient, or else white-box tests should be included to increase the level of confidence in the software. Further study will help determine which course of action is most appropriate.

Indeed, the organization's testing policy may change now that the company's software is being used to track controlled substances. However, changes to testing policy should only be made after a risk analysis has been carried out. Only then will it be possible to determine appropriate changes. For this reason, answer (a) is considered most correct.

Reference

1. Perry, W., *Effective Methods for Software Testing*, John Wiley & Sons, 2000.

A software product is in its third release. The current test effort is totally manual. Senior test engineers are assigned to test the new functionality of a release, whereas junior testers are assigned the task of manually conducting the regression test cases.

Question   Which of the following arguments does NOT support a case for automating the regression test cases?

a) Automated testing increases the precision with which a test is repeated.

b) Regression testing is more likely to be executed completely with each release of the software.

c) Automated testing can take advantage of nonworking hours.

d) Manual testing is typically less expensive than automated testing.

Answer: d

Explanation

Regression test plans contain several test cases designed to detect whether software modifications have introduced any defects into an updated system. Because these test suites are often rather lengthy, automation can increase precision, encourage completeness, and take advantage of nonworking hours. Therefore, answers (a), (b), and (c) indeed support automated regression testing.

Test automation can improve precision because there is some chance that a human error will occur each time a long test suite is run manually. Release schedules are sometimes very tight, so test automation can help project managers overcome the imprudent temptation to scale back regression testing in order to meet projected schedule milestones. Moreover, these tests can be run overnight, an option that might not be available or practical when tests are performed manually.

On the other hand, answer (d) is difficult to evaluate quantitatively. Automated tests are typically rather time-consuming and expensive to set up (some estimates say that it can take up to ten times longer to set up an automated test than to run it manually). In the case of regression testing, in which each test is likely to be run more than 11 times, this can be a justifiable investment. Nevertheless, it is difficult to measure which type of testing is "less expensive," especially when various cost and scheduling factors (such as supporting software and license fees, production during nonworking hours, and test case maintenance) are considered. Moreover, the decision to use automated or manual testing should not be based on cost alone. Each technique has strengths and weaknesses. The two techniques are best regarded as complementary, not competing, approaches.

References

1. Beizer, B., *Black-Box Testing: Techniques for Functional Testing of Software and Systems*, John Wiley & Sons, 1995.

2. Kaner, C., Bach, J., and Pettichord, B., *Lessons Learned in Software Testing*, John Wiley & Sons, 2002.

Your company purchased a new financial accounting package from a vendor last year. The system has been in use for several months. Now that you are starting to generate your end-of-year reports, you start to notice anomalies. In order to track down the problems, you retrieve last year's input data and resulting reports to compare with the new system. When you run the new system on the old data, it produces different results than it should in a few cases. You need to identify which components of the new system are at fault, but you do not have access to the source code of the system.

Question Which of the following testing methods should be used?

       I.   Branch testing

      II. Boundary value analysis

    III. Cyclomatic testing

    IV. Equivalence partitioning

     V. Mutation testing

a)   I, III, and IV

b)   II, and IV

c)   II, III, and V

d)   I, II, and IV

Answer: b

Explanation

Since the source code is unavailable, we are limited to black-box techniques. Conducting white-box testing will not be possible.

Boundary value analysis and equivalence partitioning are two black-box techniques involving strategically chosen inputs. Branch and cyclomatic testing are two white-box techniques based on program logic and flow graphs. Mutation testing is a form of fault injection; it requires modifications to the source code. Without access to source code, neither mutation testing nor white-box testing can be performed. For these reasons, (b) is the right answer.

References

1. Gao, J.Z., Tsao, H.-S. J., and Wu, Y., *Testing and Quality Assurance for Component-Based Software*, Artech House, 2003.

2. Pressman, R., *Software Engineering: A Practitioner's Approach*, McGraw-Hill, 2005.

3. Zhu, H., Hall, P.A.V., and May, J.H.R. *Software Unit Test Coverage and Adequacy*. ACM Computing Surveys, Vol. 29, No. 4, December, 1997.

A new organization is working on its first product, an online service to enable instructional videos to be viewed on-demand. The company also intends to partner with other companies so that prospective customers can also buy the needed project or lesson materials needed to complete a project on one of the instructional videos (e.g., woodworking or cake decorating). The product is currently in the testing phase.

Question The graphical user interface needs to be tested for acceptance. The inexperienced testers in the group are unsure of how to proceed in order to meet this need. What is the BEST guidance that the experienced leader of the test team can provide?

a) Run a set of black-box tests on the interface, according to tasks that the user needs to complete.

b) Run a set of black-box tests that test the exceptional cases of product use.

c) The unit tests test the user interface sufficiently; no other tests are possible.

d) No testing methods exist that can test a user interface. The user needs to just use the product.

Answer: a

Explanation

Answers (c) and (d) are blatantly incorrect. Procedures and tools for user interface testing do exist. Unit testing is not designed to find errors in the user interface.

This leaves answers (a) and (b), the crux of the difference being whether normal or exceptional use should be emphasized. Neither normal nor exceptional uses should be excluded from testing altogether, but it certainly makes sense that (assuming limited testing resources), we begin with the normal operations of the software. After all, functions that users are most likely to utilize need to be tested, at the least.

One key aspect of this question is the intended use of the product: on-demand video in the educational domain. If this were a more safety-critical project (such as an application from the transportation, medical, or military domains), then it would be vital to test both normal and exceptional uses of the system. Some costly and even deadly software bugs have been traced to unpropitious conditions and atypical interactions with the user interface.

References

1. Edgar, S.L., *Morality and Machines: Perspectives on Computer Ethics*, Jones and Bartlett Publishers, 2003.

2. Hutcheson, M.L., *Software Testing Fundamentals*, John Wiley & Sons, 2003.

3. van Vliet, H. *Software Engineering: Principles and Practice*, John Wiley & Sons, 2000.

A new organization is working on its first product, an online service to enable instructional videos to be viewed on-demand. The company also intends to partner with other companies so that prospective customers can also buy the needed project or lesson materials needed to complete a project on one of the instructional videos (e.g., woodworking or cake decorating). The product is currently in the testing phase.

Question Management has mandated that all testing will be automated in order to achieve better quality in a shorter period of time. The testing team leader has stated in meetings that the team needs resources to improve the testing process, which she says is currently ineffective. Management responds with the argument that automation will improve testing. What is the BEST argument AGAINST automating all testing for the product?

a) Automated regression testing finds a minority of the bugs. Reviews and inspections have the potential for detecting more defects.

b) The testing will not improve since the automation will only result in running bad tests faster.

c) Fewer tests will need to be run more often. The tool can run these tests faster.

d) Automated verification of testing results has limitations that can be addressed by manual testing.

Answer: b

Explanation

Automation can improve the accuracy of regression testing with dramatic speedup, while alleviating some of the tedium and unpredictability associated with manually executing lengthy test plans. Nevertheless, automation alone cannot improve the quality of testing. Testing is only as good as the test plan itself; automation can improve efficiency, but not effectiveness.

Answer (c) is a valid argument FOR automation, so it cannot be the correct answer to this question. Answer (a) may be factual, but it certainly does not argue against automated testing, because reviews and inspections can be performed in conjunction with automated testing. Answer (d) is a truism, but more weakly related than answer (b) to the problem described in the scenario.

References

1. Kaner, C., Bach, J., and Pettichord, B., *Lessons Learned in Software Testing*, John Wiley & Sons, 2002.

2. Hayes, L.G., *Automated Testing Handbook*, Software Testing Institute, 1996.

Area editor: John Reisner

VI. Software Maintenance

A) Software maintainability
B) Software maintenance process
C) Software maintenance measurement
D) Software maintenance planning
E) Software maintenance management
F) Software maintenance documentation

Question The software maintenance team at Acme Systems has to classify the type of maintenance associated with each problem found in their software release. They decide to use the IEEE Standard for Software Maintenance (IEEE Std 1219-1998). Based upon this information, which of the following would NOT be a valid maintenance type?

a) Regressive
b) Adaptive
c) Perfective
d) Emergency

Answer: a

Explanation

IEEE Standard 1219-1998 lists four types of maintenance: adaptive, corrective, perfective, and emergency. Regression testing is performed after software maintenance activities, but "regressive" is not a valid maintenance type.

References

1. Grubb, P., and Takang, A.A., *Software Maintenance: Concepts and Practice*, World Scientific, 2003.

2. IEEE Std 1219-1998, *IEEE Standard for Software Maintenance*, IEEE, 1998.

3. Pigoski, T.M., *Practical Software Maintenance*, John Wiley & Sons, 1997.

Suppose that a class named Array exists in a company's core object-oriented class library. The class Matrix is implemented as a subclass of Array. Later, new applications arise in which the supporting matrices are sparse and therefore for which an array representation is wasteful.

Question How can current design and implementation best be extended to support sparse matrices and more gracefully evolve to support other, future matrix types and new underlying representations?

a) Create a SparseMatrix class as a subclass of Matrix.

b) Create SparseMatrix as a new, direct subclass of Array.

c) Refactor the current inheritance relationship using delegation.

d) Rewrite the Array class.

Answer: c

Explanation

Although Array may have been an appropriate superclass for Matrix, an array is not a fitting parent for a SparseMatrix class. Given the stated goal of better supporting other types of matrices in the future, it would be best to relax the relationship between the array and the matrices, and this can be accomplished using the refactoring technique, replacing inheritance by delegation. Moreover, this approach leaves the original array class intact, so that any code using the array class will not need to be reconfigured.

References

1. Fowler, M., *Refactoring: Improving the Design of Existing Code*, Addison-Wesley, 1999.

2. McConnell, S., *Code Complete*, Microsoft Press, 2004.

Question According to IEEE Std 1219-1998 (Standard for Software Maintenance), a defined maintenance process for implementing a change to a software artifact includes all of the following EXCEPT:

a) Analysis

b) Implementation

c) Indemnification

d) Design

Answer: c

Explanation

The IEEE maintenance process model referenced in the question includes the following steps:

- Problem identification and classification
- Analysis
- Design
- Implementation
- Regression/system testing
- Acceptance testing
- Delivery

References

1. IEEE Std 1219-1998, *IEEE Standard for Software Maintenance*, IEEE, 1998.

2. Pigoski, T.M., *Practical Software Maintenance*, John Wiley & Sons, 1997.

Question Adaptive Maintenance is defined as:

a) The modification of a software product after delivery to keep a computer program usable in a changed or changing environment

b) The reactive modification of a software product performed after delivery to correct discovered faults

c) The unscheduled corrective maintenance performed to keep a system operational

d) The modification of a software product after delivery to improve performance or maintainability

Answer: a

Explanation

Answer (a) describes adaptive maintenance. Answer (b) describes corrective maintenance. Answer (c) describes emergency maintenance. Answer (d) describes perfective maintenance.

References

1. IEEE Std 1219-1998, *IEEE Standard for Software Maintenance*, IEEE, 1998.

2. Pigoski, T.M., *Practical Software Maintenance*, John Wiley & Sons, 1997.

Frank, a software developer, has been put in charge of maintaining a menu planning system used in hospitals to plan nutritionally well-balanced meals (breakfast, lunch, dinner, and snacks) for a variety of different diets (e.g., low salt, diabetic, etc.) The menu planning system was first written in 1984.

Question   Frank's manager has asked him to identify the main factors that affect the cost of maintaining the system. Which of the following are such factors?

> I.   Quality of system documentation
>
> II. System development time
>
> III. Number of concurrent users
>
> IV. Age of the program

a) I and IV only
b) I and III only
c) II and III only
d) II and IV only

Answer: a

Explanation

Several factors can be considered when estimating a system's maintenance cost. Some of these factors include system size, complexity, understandability, modularity, cohesiveness, and the quality of the system documentation.

Answer I, quality of system documentation, can directly affect maintenance costs. If a system is poorly documented, it is generally more difficult to understand, and understandability influences maintainability.

Answer II, system development time, is an inconclusive indicator of maintainability. Although it is true that larger and more complex systems generally take more time to develop, this is an indirect inference. It would be better to measure system size directly than attempt to infer size based on system development time. Moreover, an increased development time may imply a larger system (which would adversely affect maintenance costs), or it might indicate that more time was spent on system documentation (which would ease the maintenance effort).

Likewise, Answer III, number of concurrent users, does not affect maintainability estimates. Although it may be true that concurrency itself can increase system complexity, the number of concurrent users is not an accurate metric for predicting maintainability. Whether or not a system is concurrent may affect complexity (and, by extension, maintainability), but the actual number of users is not likely have an impact on maintenance costs.

Answer IV, age of the program, may affect maintenance costs for several reasons. It is not uncommon for systems to experience gradual degradation in maintainability after undergoing several revisions. Several factors contribute to this degradation, including widening gaps between system documentation and code, and erosion of original system quality. Such an argument may imply that number of revisions would be a better metric than system age; however, age affects maintainability in other ways as well. Quite often, legacy systems were constructed using now-outdated tools, methodologies, languages, and developmental hardware. As such, they can become extremely expensive to maintain. Since the system in question was originally deployed more than two decades ago, age is certainly a significant consideration in this instance.

References

1. Bell, D., *Software Engineering: A Programming Approach*, Addison-Wesley, 2000.

2. Pigoski, T.M., *Practical Software Maintenance*, John Wiley & Sons, 1997.

3. Polo, M., Piattini, M., and Ruiz, F. (eds.), *Advances in Software Maintenance Management*, Idea Group Publishing, 2003.

4. Sommerville, I., *Software Engineering*, Addison-Wesley, 2004.

A design team is working on the design of a payroll system. The system is being revised to accommodate new features that the customer desires. Previous versions of the design were not well documented, and the team is taking advantage of the current revision to document the new design.

Question During the test planning process, the testing team discussed how to test maintainability of the system. Which of the following measures BEST correlates to the system's maintainability after delivery?

a) The cyclomatic complexity

b) The number of requirements that have passed inspection

c) The number of proposed changes to the system

d) The degree of coverage testing conducted

Answer: a

Explanation

All of these measures affect system maintenance, but only one correlates to system maintainability.

The attained degree of test coverage may affect the correctness of the released system. Although inadequate testing may lead to a higher number of corrective maintenance requests, it will not have a significant impact on the actual maintainability of the software.

Similarly, a large number of proposed changes might foreshadow a high number of perfective maintenance requests in the future, but these requests do not affect the maintainability of the software product.

Poorly written requirements often lead to rework, thereby intensifying the maintenance effort, but, once again, these problems do not affect the maintainability of the software itself.

The complexity of the software product, on the other hand, affects its maintainability. There is a direct correlation between the complexity and understandability of software and the effort required to maintain it. Two oft-cited metrics used to measure code readability and complexity are Halstead's measures and McCabe's cyclomatic complexity metric, the latter of which is referenced in this question.

References

1. Gao, J.Z., Tsao, H.-S. J., and Wu, Y., *Testing and Quality Assurance for Component-Based Software*, Artech House, 2003.

2. Culbertson, R., Brown, C., and Cobb, G., *Rapid Testing*, Prentice-Hall, 2002.

3. Sommerville, I., *Software Engineering*, Addison-Wesley, 2004.

Area editor: Susan K. Land

VII. *Software Configuration Management*

1	VII	SOFTWARE CONFIGURATION MANAGEMENT
	B	Software configuration identification

Question Software configuration management involves identifying the configuration of the software

a) Prior to the beginning of the life cycle
b) At the beginning of the life cycle only
c) At predefined points of time during the life cycle
d) At the end of the life cycle only

Answer: c

Explanation

As described by IEEE Std 12207.0, Industry Implementation of International Standard ISO/IEC 12207: 1995 Standard for Information Technology—Software Life Cycle Processes, the organizational processes supporting configuration management activities must be defined and tailored to support individual projects. The standard states:

"The Configuration Management Process is a process of applying administrative and technical procedures throughout the software life cycle to: identify, define, and baseline software items in a system; control modifications and releases of the items; record and report the status of the items and modification requests; ensure the completeness, consistency, and correctness of the items; and control storage, handling, and delivery of the items."

The standard requires that a configuration management plan be established for each project and that each plan include a description of all relevant procedures, schedules, and responsibilities. Since the standard requires that the procedures described in the plan be carried out throughout the life cycle, the only correct answer is (c).

References

1. IEEE Std 12207.0, *Industry Implementation of International Standard ISO/IEC 12207: 1995 Standard for Information Technology—Software Life Cycle Processes*, IEEE Press, 1996.

| 2 | VII | SOFTWARE CONFIGURATION MANAGEMENT |
| | A | Management of SCM process |

Question What is the primary responsibility of software configuration management?

a) Analysis of change
b) Definition of change
c) Number of changes
d) Control of change

Answer: d

Explanation

As described by IEEE Std 12207.0, Industry Implementation of International Standard ISO/IEC 12207: 1995 Standard for Information Technology—Software Life Cycle Processes:

"The Configuration Management Process is a process of applying administrative and technical procedures throughout the software life cycle to: identify, define, and baseline software items in a system; control modifications and releases of the items; record and report the status of the items and modification requests; ensure the completeness, consistency, and correctness of the items; and control storage, handling, and delivery of the items."

As defined by IEEE Std 610.12, IEEE Standard Glossary of Software Engineering Terminology, Configuration Management is:

"A discipline applying technical and administrative direction and surveillance to: identify and document the functional and physical characteristics of a configuration item, control changes to those characteristics, record and report change processing and implementation status, and verify compliance with specified requirements."

Answer (d), *control of change*, is the only choice consistent with the two standards.

References

1. IEEE Std 12207.0, *Industry Implementation of International Standard ISO/IEC 12207: 1995 Standard for Information Technology—Software Life Cycle Processes*, IEEE Press, 1996.

2. IEEE Std 610.12, *IEEE Standard Glossary of Software Engineering Terminology*, 1990 (R2002), IEEE Press, 2002.

Question A software configuration audit should include which of the following?

I. *Review of configuration management library system*

II. *Verification of compliance with applicable procedures*

III. *Completeness of software baseline library*

IV. *Correctness of software baseline library*

a) II, III, IV only
b) I, II only
c) III, IV only
d) I, II, III, and IV

Answer: c

Explanation

There are two types of configuration audits: functional and physical. As defined by the IEEE Standard Glossary of Terms (IEEE Std 610.12):

"Functional configuration audit (FCA): An audit conducted to verify that the development of a configuration item has been completed satisfactorily, that the item has achieved the performance and functional characteristics specified in the functional or allocated configuration identification, and that its operational and support documents are complete and satisfactory."

"Physical configuration audit (PCA): An audit conducted to verify that a configuration item, as built, conforms to the technical documentation that defines it."

To further clarify, a functional configuration audit (FCA) for a software item verifies that test results indicate the successful completion of all requirements associated with the release. All test results are traced back to related functional requirements. The FCA verifies and validates that all requirements have been met and are included in the product baseline. A physical configuration audit (PCA) for a software item is the formal examination that establishes that the software, as built, conforms to the design and construction process or technical documentation that defines it. It is performed during the production and deployment phase and focuses on production suitability. The PCA verifies that the related design documentation matches the design of the deliverable configuration item.

Neither of these configuration audits requires that the configuration management system, or its supporting procedures, be verified or validated.

References

1. IEEE Std 610.12, *IEEE Standard Glossary of Software Engineering Terminology*, 1990 (R2002), IEEE Press, 2002.

2. IEEE Std 12207.0, *Industry Implementation of International Standard ISO/IEC 12207: 1995 Standard for Information Technology—Software Life Cycle Processes*, IEEE Press, 1996.

3. IEEE Std 828, *IEEE Standard for Software Configuration Management Plans*, IEEE Press, 1998.

Early development of a new product development project proceeded smoothly. Team members were given individual responsibility for components of the final system, and they developed their code independently. The integration phase was the first time that different code modules were brought together, but clear specifications enabled this phase to complete quickly.

Now that testing is underway, the team is thrashing: lots of work seems to be going on, but very little progress is being made. In particular, bug fixes often introduce new bugs, so the total bug count just keeps increasing.

Question   What steps should be taken to improve the team's performance?

    I.   *Implement version control*

    II.   *Establish a baseline for all the code*

    III.   *Require that only the module's original author perform all changes to a module*

    IV.   *Perform a configuration audit for each proposed change*

    V.   *Send configuration status reports to all team members*

a)   II, III only

b)   I, III only

c)   I, II, IV only

d)   I, II, V only

Answer: d

Explanation

Configuration control helps to ensure that all changes to an established baseline are controlled. Establishing a product baseline and subsequent version control can act as enablers to control a changing product. Requiring that the author perform all fixes may introduce bottlenecks when one module needs several changes. If a baseline is placed under effective configuration control, the changes can be distributed among other team members in support of a more rapid response.

Team members need to know when, and how, modules are being changed. Physical configuration audits may be used to establish a product (production system) baseline. However, configuration audits during the development phase are an oversight method and will not ensure that developers know about changes that are occurring. Configuration-status accounting maintains and records the status of each baseline and its history. The reports generated from this status accounting can provide valuable information to the individual team members.

References

1. Horch, J.W., *Practical Guide to Software Quality Management*, 2nd ed., Artech House, 2003.

2. Pressman, R., *Software Engineering: A Practitioner's Approach*, 6th ed., McGraw-Hill, 2005.

3. Sodhi, J. and Sodhi, P., *Managing IT Systems Requirements*, Management Concepts, 2003.

Area editor: Susan K. Land

VIII. Software Engineering Management

Question Paul has drafted a software project management plan. Which of the following items should be discussed in this plan?

       I.   *Schedule*

      II. *Budget*

     III. *Requirements*

     IV. *Staffing*

a)   I, III, IV only

b)   I, II, III only

c)   I, II, IV only

d)   I, II, III, IV

Answer: c

Explanation

IEEE Standard 1058 is the IEEE Standard for Software Project Management Plans (SPMP). This IEEE software engineering standard specifies the format and content of SPMPs. However, it does not specify the exact techniques to be used in the development of an SPMP. The expectation is that each organization using this standard will develop a set of practices and procedures that provide detailed guidance for the preparation and update of their unique SPMPs. This standard specifically requires that the schedule, budget, and staffing be identified as part of the SPMP.

Reference

1. IEEE Std 1058-1998, *IEEE Standard for Software Project Management Plans*, IEEE Press, 1998.

Question Mary is tasked with developing a schedule for the ABC Project. She has two dates indicating project milestones as well as a specified completion date. According to IEEE Std 1490-1998(2002), these types of project constraints are known as:

a) Customer constraints

b) Budget constraints

c) Interface constraints

d) Time constraints

Answer: d

Explanation

IEEE 1490, which is published as a guide, is an adoption of the Project Management Institute's (PMI) Guide to the Project Management Body of Knowledge (PMBOK). Both of these documents identify the required dates for project milestones and completion as the two major categories of time constraints. These categories represent imposed dates and dates indicating key events or major milestones.

References

1. Project Management Institute, *A Guide to the Project Management Body of Knowledge (PMBOK Guide)*, PMI Press, 2000.

2. IEEE Std 1490-2003, *IEEE Guide—Adoption of PMI Standard—A Guide to the Project Management Body of Knowledge*, IEEE Press, 2003.

Question The following are characteristics of a milestone EXCEPT:

a) Composed of tasks
b) Completion criteria
c) Scheduled
d) Measurable

Answer: a

Explanation

The Guide to the Project Management Body of Knowledge (PMBOK) describes the generally accepted knowledge within the profession of project management. This document describes a milestone as any significant event in the project, usually the completion of a major deliverable. A milestone may be defined by its associated completion criteria, where it appears on the schedule, and how its completion will be measured. A milestone may be composed of tasks, but may also be associated with specific events. Milestones, as defined by the PMBOK, are not limited to being defined as a composition of tasks. For example, a third-party delivery of required functionality is a milestone event in the project schedule that is not a composition of project tasks.

Reference

1. Project Management Institute (PMI), *A Guide to the Project Management Body of Knowledge (PMBOK)*, Project Management Institute, 2000.

Question   According to the IEEE Std 1058-1998, a work task is best described as:

a)   A product that has been formally reviewed and accepted by the stakeholders

b)   A unique name and identifier that has been placed under configuration control

c)   The smallest unit of work subject to management accountability

d)   A tangible item produced during the process of developing or modifying software

Answer: c

Explanation

IEEE Standard 1058 is the IEEE Standard for Software Project Management Plans (SPMP). This standard defines a work task as:

"The smallest unit of work subject to management accountability. A work task must be small enough to allow adequate planning and control of a software project, but large enough to avoid micro-management. The specification of work to be accomplished in completing a work task should be documented in a work package. Related work tasks should be grouped to form supporting processes and work activities."

This IEEE Software Engineering Standard specifies the format and content of SPMPs. However, it does not specify the exact techniques to be used in the development of an SPMP. The expectation is that each organization using this standard will develop a set of practices and procedures that provide detailed guidance for the preparation and update of their unique SPMPs.

Reference

1. IEEE Std 1058-1998, *IEEE Standard for Software Project Management Plans*, IEEE Press, 1998.

An engineer is developing a Web presentation layer for a mission-critical project. The technology chosen for the presentation layer is making it difficult to implement the user interface design. The engineer reads about a new technology for creating the type of Web interface the project needs. It is decided that a rapid prototype will be created to perform an initial evaluation of the new technology.

Question Which of the following criteria is the LEAST important when doing the prototype?

a) Exercising the entire breadth of functionality

b) Simulating the operational environment

c) Exercising critical functionality

d) Stepping through source code with a debugger

Answer: d

Explanation

Prototypes can range from storyboard mockups to a working partial system. It is important that all stakeholders understand the goal for the prototype and the resources available in support of the effort. At its most basic level, a prototype is some type of concrete, but partial, implementation of system design. The result of a prototyping effort should be changes to, or refinement of, the design, not a deployable product.

There are two fundamental drivers when determining the goals for a prototyping effort: Cost and end-product viability. How much will the system cost? Is the goal product reuse? These drivers will affect the amount of exercised functionality, the level of operational simulation, and which critical functionality should be exercised. Prototypes will not be error free, and in many cases may not even be based in software code.

References

1. Rosson, M.B. and Carroll, J.M., *Usability Engineering: Scenario-Based Development of Human-Computer Interaction*, Morgan Kaufmann Publishers, 2002.

2. McConnell. S., *Rapid Development*, Microsoft Press, 1996.

Jo is developing a web presentation layer for a mission-critical project with a challenging schedule. The project manager, who does not have a technical background, is always pressing for ways to reduce schedule risk. The project is following a staged-delivery life cycle. Requirements and architecture are completed, along with the first stage that delivered the initial database. Vertical slices of functionality are now being developed incrementally. The technology chosen for the presentation layer is making it difficult to implement the user interface design. Jo has just read about a new technology for creating the type of Web interface her project needs.

Question   Adopting a new technology at this stage of a project introduces the following risks:

    I.   *Increased integration effort and time*

    II. *Decreased usability*

    III. *Increased testing effort and time*

    IV. *Lower system performance*

    V. *Lower system reliability*

a)   I and III only
b)   I, II, and III only
c)   I, III, IV, and V only
d)   I, II, III, IV, and V

Answer: c

Explanation

New software technologies and methodologies are continuously being introduced. Many promise cheaper, faster, and more reliable software development results. In some cases, adopting new technologies and/or methodologies will actually make things worse. Specifically, the introduction of a new technology, or new methodology, into a project can introduce risks associated with integration, testing, performance, and reliability. The new technology/methodology may conflict with existing organizational or technical constraints. The addition of a new technology at any point in the lifecycle increases risk, but particular attention must be paid after development has begun.

Reference

1. McConnell, S., *Rapid Development*, Microsoft Press, 1996.

Jo is developing a Web presentation layer for a mission-critical project with a challenging schedule. The project manager, who does not have a technical background, is always pressing for ways to reduce schedule risk. The project is following a staged-delivery life cycle. Requirements and architecture are completed, along with the first stage that delivered the initial database. Vertical slices of functionality are now being developed incrementally. The technology chosen for the presentation layer is making it difficult to implement the user interface design. Jo has just read about a new technology for creating the type of Web interface her project needs.

Question   It appears that the new technology can drastically cut the interface development time. At this point Jo should:

a)   Take initiative and employ the technology on the project.

b)   Discuss the technology with other developers and employ it if there is agreement.

c)   Discuss changes to the project plan with the project manager.

d)   Postpone using the technology until a future project.

Answer: c

Explanation

Coordination with the project manager is critical since the manager would have visibility into all associated project activities that may be impacted by a software change. Management should be informed so that they may evaluate any risk associated with deploying a new technology. If the new technology is adopted, all associated changes to project planning will need to be evaluated as well.

Reference

1. Davis, A., *201 Principles of Software Development*, McGraw-Hill, 1995.

Jo is developing a Web presentation layer for a mission-critical project with a challenging schedule. The project manager, who does not have a technical background, is always pressing for ways to reduce schedule risk. The project is following a staged-delivery life cycle. Requirements and architecture are completed, along with the first stage that delivered the initial database. Vertical slices of functionality are now being developed incrementally. The technology chosen for the presentation layer is making it difficult to implement the user interface design. Jo has just read about a new technology for creating the type of Web interface her project needs.

Question Of the following, which are not considered effective steps to evaluate the new technology?

a) Reading articles and user groups about it
b) Comparing product literature to similar products
c) Building test prototypes
d) Trying it out by building a small feature for the next release

Answer: d

Explanation

Reading articles and user groups is a common way for a developer to learn about a new technology. Similarly, developers generally compare product literature for a new technology to literature for similar products.

A prototype is a concrete but partial implementation of a system design. Prototypes may be created to explore many questions during system development—for example, system reliability, bandwidth consumption, or hardware compatibility.

Prototypes can be developed in service of different goals—to discover or refine user requirements, to explore design ideas, to test specific open issues, and to explore early implementation efforts or new technologies. A new or unknown technology could be prototyped before it is incorporated into the system being built. However, this prototyped technology should not be deployed in the released product. The integration of the new technology into the released product should occur only following the evaluation of the prototyping effort. Thus (d) is the correct answer.

References

1. Pfleeger, S., *Software Engineering,* 2nd ed., Prentice-Hall, 2001.

2. Sommerville, I., *Software Engineering. 4th ed.,* Addison-Wesley, 1992.

3. Rosson, M.B. and Carroll, J.M., *Usability Engineering: Scenario-Based Development of Human-Computer Interaction*, Morgan Kaufmann Publishers, 2002.

A cross-functional maintenance team of five people is responsible for adding a new feature to an existing system (one person is project manager, one is a business analyst, two are developers, and one is a tester). The project manager got the team together to create a bottom-up estimate of effort for delivering that feature. They held a meeting and used expert judgment to break down the work into a set of task buckets and estimated the effort for the detailed work tasks in each one. The table below is the documentation of the estimate:

Task	Estimated Effort (hours)
Elicit Requirements	15
Analyze, Capture, and Model Requirements	30
Design	35
Construct X	20
Construct Y	35
Construct Z	25
System Test	30
Integration Test with System	5
Rollout and Cutover	10
Management Overhead	40
Total	245

All four team members are involved in other projects, so their participation in this effort will be part-time. Taking into account staff availability, the project manager creates a schedule for delivering the feature. The project manager decides to use earned value to track the progress of the project. Team members track their time against the different tasks.

Question The project manager tracks the progress of the execution against the estimate. The best ways for her to report the earned value of the project is:

I. Actual hours vs. planned hours for each task

II. Percentage complete for each task

III. Completion of each task

IV. Start and stop dates for each task

V. Breakdown of staff member hours per task

a) I and IV only
b) II and IV only
c) II and V only
d) I and III only

Answer: d

Explanation

Earned value management (EVM) can seem complex, but it has a simple foundation. Project planning generates a schedule and a budget. Project plan execution generates real data, resulting in an actual schedule and an actual budget. EVM is one way to assess the differences between these planned and actual schedules and budgets. EVM evaluates project progress in terms of diagnostic metrics that are related to these schedules and. The three principal metrics for EVM are:

Budgets

		Planned Expenses	Actual Expenses
Schedules	Planned Schedule	Planned Value (BCWS)	
	Actual Schedule	Earned Value (BCWP)	Actual Cost (ACWP)

Of the combinations of answers presented, the knowledge of actual vs. planned effort is critical, as is the knowledge that the task is complete (actual). The other information combinations are useful, but are not related to tracking the earned value for the project.

The value of EVM has been debated extensively. It can represent quite a bit of overhead, and may be prohibitive for some projects. EVM should not be dismissed casually, since it can accurately predict project budget overruns as early as 15 percent of the way through a problem project.

Reference

1. Kendrick, T., *The Project Management Tool Kit: 100 Tips and Techniques for Getting the Job Done Right*, American Management Association, 2004.

A cross-functional maintenance team of five people is responsible for adding a new feature to an existing system (one person is project manager, one is a business analyst, two are developers, and one is a tester). The project manager got the team together to create a bottom-up estimate of effort for delivering that feature. They held a meeting and used expert judgment to break down the work into a set of task buckets and estimated the effort for the detailed work tasks in each one. The table below is the documentation of the estimate:

Task	Estimated Effort (hours)
Elicit Requirements	15
Analyze, Capture, and Model Requirements	30
Design	35
Construct X	20
Construct Y	35
Construct Z	25
System Test	30
Integration Test with System	5
Rollout and Cutover	10
Management Overhead	40
Total	245

All four team members are involved in other projects, so their participation in this effort will be part-time. Taking into account staff availability, the project manager creates a schedule for delivering the feature. The project manager decides to track the progress of the execution against the estimate. Team members track their time against the different tasks.

Question The following would be significant improvements to the estimate EXCEPT

a) Using time instead of effort
b) Documenting the assumptions behind each task
c) Using low and high effort instead of a single number
d) Basing the estimate on historical data

Answer: a

Explanation

There are many useful techniques available for time and effort estimation. Bottom-up estimation involves the identification and estimation of each individual component separately. The results of these individual estimates are then combined to produce an estimate for the entire project.

Process and project metrics can provide historical perspective and powerful input for the generation of quantitative estimates. The previous experiences of all people involved in the project can provide much help as estimates are developed and reviewed. The documentation of all assumptions providing the basis for the estimates can add value during review or discussion.

Effort is usually estimated in terms of the person-hours, person-days, or person-months that need to be consumed to create the software. Schedule is derived from the effort estimate, the number of team members, and the extent to which project life cycle activities are independent of each other. It is often useful to have participants identify low and high estimated values. The mean of these values will often provide a more realistic estimate.

It has been said many times that estimation is more of an art than a science. It is important to remember that the application of common sense, along with the use of data from past performance history, are key to successful estimations.

Reference

1. Pandian, C. R., *Software Metrics: A Guide to Planning, Analysis, and Application*, Auerbach Publications, 2004.

Question Consider a military system that is to be developed in the C programming language. An estimation of the function points in the system has been performed, resulting in about 8500 function points. Which of the following statements are TRUE:

I. *If this same system would be developed in Ada the number of function points would be different.*

II. *Considering a productivity ratio of 1.9 function points per staff-month, the total effort for this project is estimated to be about 4500 staff-months.*

III. *The number of function points indicated refers only to the construction phase of the system.*

a) II, III only

b) III only

c) I, III only

d) II only

Answer: d

Explanation

In the late 1970s, IBM assigned one of its employees, Allan Albrecht, to develop an approach to the estimation of software effort. The result of his efforts was the function point technique. In the early 1980s, the function point technique was refined and a counting manual was produced by IBM's GUIDE organization. The International Function Point Users Group (IFPUG) was founded in the late 1980s. This organization produced its own Counting Practices Manual (Release 4.0 appeared in 1994).

Function points are a measure of the size of computer applications and the projects that build them. The size is measured from a functional, or user, point of view. It is independent of the computer language, development methodology, technology, or capability of the project team used to develop the application. The fact that Albrecht originally used it to predict effort is simply a consequence of the fact that size is usually the primary driver of development effort. The function points measured size.

It is important to stress what function points do NOT measure. Function points are not a perfect measure of effort to develop an application or of its business value, although the project size as measured by function points is typically an important indicator.

References

1. Jones, T.C., *Estimating Software Costs*, McGraw-Hill, 1998.

2. International Function Point Users Group, http://www.ifpug.org/.

3. *Function Point Counting Practices Manual*, International Function Point Users Group, http://www.ifpug.org/publications, 2004.

Question Catherine has elicited from her client the use cases that a software system her organization is developing should provide. The time and resources available for the first product delivery are limited, and they allow just for the implementation of part of the system. Catherine will have to choose a set of use cases to tackle in the first delivery. From the following use case qualities, which ones would increase the probability of a use case of being chosen for the first delivery?

    I.   *Represents a high risk for the success of the project*

    II.   *Offers an opportunity for creativity*

    III.   *Directly supports increased revenue for the client*

    IV.   *Has a significant impact on the architectural design*

a)   I, III, IV only

b)   II, III, IV only

c)   II, III only

d)   I, II only

Answer: a

Explanation

In the language of UML, a type of user is called an actor, and a written model of the way that the actor uses different parts of the system is called a use case. Use cases shift the focus of requirements development. The traditional approach is to ask users what they want the system to do. The use case approach requires that users describe what they need to accomplish. All participants must ensure that each use case lies within the defined project scope before accepting it into the requirements baseline. A use case is a representation of user requirements and I, III, and IV are qualities that increase the ranking of a use case for deciding whether it is to be assigned to development cycles. The development of staff creativity is not directly relevant to the customer's needs.

References

1. Larman, C., *Applying UML and Patterns*, Prentice-Hall, 1998.

2. Wiegers, K., *Software Requirements,* 2nd ed., Microsoft Press, 2003.

Question A test team lead at a small software company has decided to use a commercially available software-problem-tracking product rather than developing one internally. The rationale for this choice could include which of the following?

 I. *It is readily available.*

 II. *Buying a commercial product means the company does not need to develop a problem-tracking process.*

 III. *The company does not have to use internal resources to build and test an internal tool.*

 IV. *The vendor's user groups can provide valuable information on the system, tracking models, technology, and so on.*

a) I, II only

b) I, II, III only

c) I, III, IV only

d) I, II, III, and IV

Answer: c

Explanation

A commercial problem-tracking product supports, but does not provide, a tracking process. According to the IEEE Standard Classification for Software Anomalies (IEEE Std 1044), The classification process is a series of activities, starting with the recognition of an anomaly through to its closure. The process is divided into four sequential steps interspersed with three administrative activities.

The sequential steps are as follows:

Step 1: Recognition

Step 2: Investigation

Step 3: Action

Step 4: Disposition

The three administrative activities applied to each sequential step are as follows:

Activity 1: Recording

Activity 2: Classifying

Activity 3: Identifying impact

Any given commercially available tracking product will support the steps and activities described above. However, individual implementing organizations should use procedures and processes that accomplish their unique objectives. This will require additional detail, may require a different sequence of steps, and should define the level of organizational involvement.

Reference

1. The Institute of Electrical and Electronics Engineers, IEEE-Std 1044-1993 (R2002) *IEEE Standard Classification for Software Anomalies*, September 2002.

Question A risk analysis group is preparing a risk assessment for a new development effort. As part of this activity, which of the following should be done?

    I.   *Risk identification*

    II.   *Risk analysis*

    III.   *Risk prioritization*

    IV.   *Risk treatment*

a)   I, II only

b)   I, II, III only

c)   I, IV only

d)   I, II, III, and IV

Answer: b

Explanation

Risk treatment is the responsibility of the technical development group. The risk analysis group may define the managerial and technical processes involving all stakeholders.

The IEEE Computer Society software engineering standard that most directly addresses this issue, the standard for Software Life Cycle Processes — Risk Management (IEEE Std-1540) states that it is the responsibility of management to decide what risk treatment should be implemented for any risk found to be unacceptable. Risk treatment plans are created for risks that require treatment. These plans are coordinated with other management plans and other ongoing activities.

References

1. The Institute of Electrical and Electronics Engineers, IEEE-Std 1540-2001 *IEEE Standard for Software Life Cycle Processes — Risk Management*, August 2003.

A technical lead is working on an iterative life cycle project that is creating a well-understood application using a technology the team has experience with. The project has 10 major use cases to implement; two have just been delivered on schedule in the first iteration. At the request of the project manager, who is concerned about the amount of effort being spent fixing defects, the lead has collected some data on quality performance during the first iteration. The data shows that planned reviews of requirements and design are not occurring. It shows that 22 defects are being detected during unit and system testing per 1000 SLOC.

Question The lead is asked to manage the risk that rework is posing to the schedule. The following would be the most effective strategy to manage this risk:

   I.   Move detection activities as far upstream as possible.

   II. Determine which areas of the system have the highest defect rates.

   III. Increase the fix rate for defects.

   IV. Rewrite the most error-prone areas.

a) I, II, and IV
b) I and III
c) II and IV
d) I, II, III, and IV

Answer: a

Explanation

III is not risk management but instead focuses on rework. I, II, and IV are all good options to reduce the probability or impact of future rework.

The *PMBOK® Guide* is built around five process groups: initiating, planning, executing, controlling, and closing. In the *PMBOK® Guide*, the processes are related as shown in the figure below. Project risk management is included in two of these groups: planning processes and controlling processes.

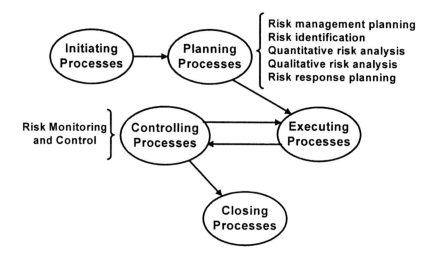

The PMBOK suggests that risk management activities be included as part of the planning processes. These planned activities will then be executed and controlled.

The data gathered for risk management activities can be analysed to determine the areas with the highest defect density ratio. The evaluation of problem areas of code can significantly reduce the risk of rework.

References

1. McConnell, S., *Rapid Development*, Microsoft Press, 1996.

2. Project Management Institute, *A Guide to the Project Management Body of Knowledge (PMBOK Guide)*, PMI Press, 2000.

A software organization is reviewing the project tracking data from its completed projects. It appeared that every project delivered its products late, with an average schedule overrun of about 25%.

Question Which of the following is the best course of action?

a) Perform causal analysis of schedule overruns.
b) Pad all future schedules by 25%.
c) Cut all future development schedules by 20%.
d) Do nothing because management will dictate delivery dates.

Answer: a

Explanation

Identifying common causes of risk or project delays may reveal opportunities to mitigate project risks. Keeping extensive project data on problems encountered in previous projects leads to process improvements.

Causal analysis is a quality-management approach to software development that uses defect data feedback from work product inspections as a means of improving the quality of development processes. The ultimate goal of causal analysis is defect prevention. The clear benefit is higher product quality and improved productivity through reductions in rework.

The software inspection process is in itself a prevention technique, but the statistics obtained from this process must be augmented with in-depth study to find out what caused the defects. The goals of causal analysis are:

- To identify development process problem areas in a systematic way

- To change the corrective-action process from one in which a single developer learns from his or her mistake to one in which all developers are familiar with, and learn from, all mistakes

- To prevent repetition of mistakes by improvement of development processes

Schedule padding is a common approach. This is not the best choice because it does not improve the organization's ability to accurately predict development time and to deliver software.

Cutting development schedules is a technique that generally further exacerbates the delivery overruns by causing shortcutting of quality-assurance activities.

Doing nothing is one of the primary excuses used by developers who are under severe schedule pressure.

Reference

1. McConnell, S., *Rapid Development*, Microsoft Press, 1996.

IX. *Software Engineering Process*

A)	Process infrastructure
B)	Process measurement
C)	Process definition
D)	Qualitative process analysis
E)	Process implementation and change

Question Software metrics should be evaluated for their utility in certain areas of application. Which one of the following areas of application should NOT be considered when evaluating the utility of software metrics?

a) Determining product complexity

b) Determining productivity of individual staff members

c) Determining when a desired state of quality has been achieved

d) Determining the validity of project processes

Answer: b

Explanation

A cardinal rule of metrics programs is, "Never use metrics for personnel evaluations." Doing so can jeopardize an entire metrics effort. If people even suspect that metrics will be used for evaluation of personnel, they will be reluctant to report findings that might be detrimental to their future careers. People will also be tempted to inflate positive indicators. Such massaging of metrics data will erase objectivity and validity, dramatically decreasing the chances that a successful metrics program will lead to improvements.

Product complexity is a valid measurement to consider; managing complexity is a legitimate software engineering goal. Moreover, complexity can be used as a predictor for error rates and maintenance efforts.

Metrics can also be used to quantitatively evaluate product quality. Deliverables can be measured to see if they in fact meet previously specified desired levels of quality.

Using a higher level of analysis, quantifiable indicators can be analyzed to determine the effectiveness of a process used by an organization or project. The use of metrics data in such analyses can more precisely confirm perceptions (or nullify misperceptions) about the efficacy of a process, and ultimately lead to continual process improvement.

Other valid areas in which metrics can be used include defect analysis, project complexity, project and product tracking, and level-of-effort baselines for future project estimation.

References

1. Christensen, M.J. and Thayer, R.H., *The Project Manager's Guide to Software Engineering's Best Practices*, IEEE Press, 2001 (Chapter 15).

2. Kan, S.H., *Metrics and Models in Software Quality Engineering*, Addison-Wesley, 1995.

3. Pandian, C.R., *Software Metrics*, Auerbach Publications, 2004.

You are the project manager leading the planning for a project to enhance a course registration and payment system for a large public university system. This domain is new to both you and your organization. One of your tasks is to select the life cycle model that is most appropriate for the project circumstances.

Question Among four common software life cycle models — waterfall, incremental, code-and-fix, and spiral — which will enable your organization to gather ongoing feedback while delivering the system in stages?

a) Waterfall
b) Spiral
c) Incremental
d) Code-and-fix

Answer: c

Explanation

In the waterfall model, the system is developed as a whole, not in phased releases. Feedback primarily occurs either after the system has been delivered, or else between adjacent phases of the life cycle. Therefore, (a) is not a good choice for a development model.

In the spiral model, each spiral loop represents a stage of the development process. During each stage, alternatives are identified and evaluated. During this evaluation, prototypes are used, implying that feedback gathering is indeed ongoing. The spiral model does not account for phased releases, however (even though it could conceivably be adopted for use in an evolutionary development environment). Therefore, (b) is not a good choice for a development model. In short, the waterfall and spiral models, in their purest form, depict a completed software system being delivered at the end of development, not meeting the phased release criterion specified in the question.

The "code-and-fix" model is an informal description of how software is written. It does not include a solid process model based on sound software engineering principles. This eliminates (d) as a good choice for a development model.

Under the Incremental model, the system is subdivided into subsystems, and the system is released in a sequence of phases, each adding more functionality to the previously released version. The earlier versions can also be used as prototypes, so the model has a built-in feedback mechanism. Therefore, the correct answer is (c).

References

1. Humphrey, W., *Managing the Software Process*, Addison-Wesley, 1989.

2. McConnell, S., *Rapid Development*, Microsoft Press, 1996.

3. McDermid, J. (ed.), *Software Engineer's Reference Book*, CRC Press, 1993.

4. Sommerville, I., *Software Engineering*, Addison-Wesley, 2004.

An engineer just started as the lead project manager at ACME. Management asked for an informal assessment to determine ACME's CMMI® level. During the course of the week, the engineer found the company has well-defined project standards. Planning and management of new projects is based on prior similar project experiences, and their processes are repeatable but not fully defined.

Question   Which of the answers below most closely describes the company's CMMI® process maturity level?

a)   Level 1
b)   Level 2
c)   Level 3
d)   Level 4

Answer: b

Explanation

In Level 3 of the CMMI® (the Defined level), a documented software engineering process plan is used for all technical and managerial activities across the organization. In Level 2 (the Managed level), software life cycle models are used for each project — planning based on similar past experiences and tracking cost and schedule — but these models and plans may differ significantly from project to project. This means the process is manageable (since it is documented), but is not defined (at the organizational level). This difference is depicted in the diagram shown below.

In a Level 2 organization, individual plans are used for each project. In a Level 3 organization, a single, documented organizational plan is tailored for each project.

Level 4 organizations have defined processes, with the addition of a metrics program, allowing the processes to be analyzed quantitatively. Metrics are collected for deliverables (product metrics) and activities (process metrics).

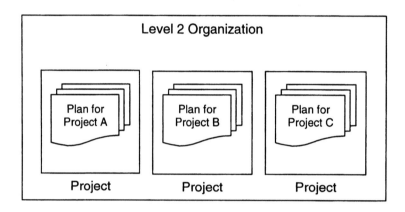

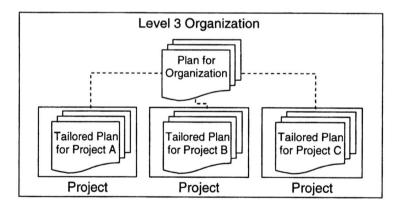

References

1. Bruegge, B., and Dutoit, A. H., *Object-Oriented Software Engineering*, Prentice-Hall, 2004.

2. Chrissis, M.B., Konrad, M., and Shrum, S., *CMMI*, Addison-Wesley, 2003.

3. Humphrey, W., *Managing the Software Process*, Addison-Wesley, 1989.

4. SEI, *Capability Maturity Model Integration (CMMI) for Software Engineering*, v.1.1 Staged Representation, Software Engineering Institute, Carnegie Mellon University, Technical Report, CMU/SEI-2002-TR-029, 2002.

The InsurePro Company develops software to support the commercial insurance industry and currently has several insurance products under development. Software development in the InsurePro Company follows one of four types of development approaches, depending on the software development project: waterfall, cleanroom, spiral, and rapid application development (RAD). A new customer-support application is proposed to allow customers to view the status of claims online. Development is expected to last at least six months depending on final requirements, resources, funding, and so on. Currently, the majority of the requirements are known, but the Customer Service Department is still unsure of final requirements in some areas, and is waiting to see initial screens of the new Web-based system before finalizing the requirements. Management has emphasized that risks must be minimized, that the project must be delivered on time, and that there is flexibility in the functionality that must be delivered.

Question   Which of the development approaches listed below would be most suitable for the InsurePro Company to reach its goals?

a)   RAD process

b)   Spiral method

c)   Waterfall model

d)   Cleanroom engineering

Answer: b

Explanation

Since risks must be minimized, we should consider models that strive to address and minimize risk. This confines the possible answers to the spiral and cleanroom engineering methodologies.

The rapid application development (RAD) process should only be used when requirements are well understood, and it is not an appropriate model to use when technical risks are high. In this instance, the requirements are not finalized, and risk minimization is paramount; therefore, RAD is not a good candidate for this project.

The unfinished requirements also weaken the case for the waterfall model. During waterfall development, it is presumed that requirements analysis is complete before development progresses into subsequent design stages, making the waterfall model a poor choice in this instance.

Cleanroom engineering aims to eliminate the injection of software errors by using statistical rigor and formal methods. Such an approach can be considered a form of risk management, particularly in safety-critical systems. However, in this case, the use of such a formal and rigorous approach seems unwarranted, particularly in light of the projected six-month development schedule.

In contrast to cleanroom engineering, the spiral method mitigates risk by using prototypes and simulations. Although cleanroom engineering emphasizes fault injection rates, the spiral method focuses on ensuring that the system will meet functional and nonfunctional expectations. This is why risk assessment and prototyping are fundamental in the spiral model, whereas formal specifications and intense statistical analysis are used in cleanroom engineering. In this case, requirements will be finalized after reviewing some screens from the Web-based system, a process that maps well to the use of software prototypes; hence, the spiral model is an ideal approach for this particular project.

References

1. Dyer, M., *The Cleanroom Approach to Quality Software Development*, John Wiley & Sons, 1992.

2. Pressman, R., *Software Engineering: A Practitioner's Approach*, 5th ed, McGraw-Hill, 2001.

Question A software development team is starting a project that has significant technological and programmatic risks. To address this, they perform requirements analysis, design, construction, integration, and testing of the riskiest portions of the system. This is an example of which of the following software development life cycle models?

a) Spiral

b) Waterfall

c) Incremental

d) Rapid prototyping

Answer: a

Explanation

The waterfall model requires project managers to consider each of the primary phases of the software life cycle: conception, requirements elicitation and analysis, preliminary and detailed design, implementation, testing, installation, and maintenance. By providing a path through all phases of the software life cycle, the model enables managers to plan a well-engineered development effort.

The incremental model accounts for the same life cycle phases, but it allows for incremental development. Illustrations of this model, therefore, show the phases in an overlapping and iterative manner, demonstrating that parallel development may occur for different versions of the system. Such an approach is often better suited for large-scale systems for which it would be very difficult to build a complete system in one large developmental pass.

Rapid prototyping emphasizes the early use of software prototypes, primarily to get early feedback from the users. This feedback can be analyzed and used during subsequent stages of development. Such an approach helps address the very real risk of developing a system that meets functional requirements, but nevertheless may leave the user rather dissatisfied with the end product.

The spiral model shares commonalities with some of the other models described. The fundamental stages of development—requirements, design, coding, testing—are depicted in the illustration of the model given on the following page. Moreover, prototyping is explicitly depicted in the model, meaning that prototypes can be used to provide early feedback. Most unique to the spiral model, however, and the very essence of the model itself, is its focus on risk-driven development. Early risk analyses are performed during each iteration of the spiral, allowing project managers to identify and address the biggest risks early in the development effort. For this reason, spiral development is the correct answer.

References

1. Pfleeger, S.L., *Software Engineering*, Prentice-Hall, 2001.

2. Schach, S.R., *Classical and Object-Oriented Software Engineering*, McGraw-Hill, 1999.

3. Sommerville, I., *Software Engineering*, Addison-Wesley, 2004.

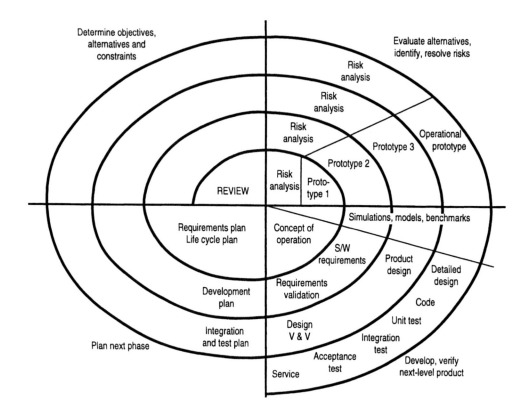

The continual analysis of risk throughout the development process is a hallmark of the spiral model.

Question A software project manager is concerned about the amount of effort being spent fixing defects. The data shows that planned reviews of requirements and design are not occurring. It shows that 22 defects per 1000 lines of code are being detected during unit and system testing. The best characterization of the defect injection rate is

a) 22 defects per 1000 lines of code

b) Less than 22 defects per 1000 lines of code

c) More than 22 defects per 1000 lines of code

d) Impossible to know with information given

Answer: c

Explanation

Defect detection rate is almost always lower than defect injection rate, because it is practically impossible to detect all errors, especially in an environment in which planned reviews during analysis and design have been skipped.

Although answer (d) is technically correct (in that we cannot determine the exact defect injection rate), answer (c) is the better answer, because we do know it is at least 22 defects per 1000 lines of code, and almost certainly higher than that.

References

1. McConnell, S., *Code Complete*, Microsoft Press, 2004.

2. McConnell, S., *Rapid Development*, Microsoft Press, 1996.

A software development company is subcontracted to reengineer an existing software system. After several releases of the software, the prime contractor comes to the subcontractor project manager with data that shows that, for the past several releases, more defects are being found during the second test cycle of a release than during the first. The prime contractor insists that the software development team is doing a poor job of fixing defects.

Question Which metric will best refute or support the prime contractor's argument?

a) Measures of the code coverage by test cycle
b) Number of test cases executed
c) Number of hours tested per test cycle
d) Number of testers per test cycle

Answer: a

Explanation

In this scenario, if more defects are found during a second test cycle than the first, then this can point to at least two problems. One of these potential problems concurs with the contractor's assertion: a poor job of fixing defects is introducing yet more defects into the system. However, to support this inference, it must be demonstrated that the first test cycle has equal or greater levels of rigor and coverage as the second. Otherwise, the real cause for more errors being found in subsequent test cycles may simply be insufficient testing in the first test cycle.

Essentially, the question is asking which metric best compares the effectiveness of the two testing cycles (comparable effectiveness must be shown before we can shift accountability from the testing process to the development team). The number of testers, testing hours, and test cases are all valid metrics for measuring testing procedures; however, they are not nearly as pertinent as code coverage metrics. Code coverage metrics are a much better way to compare two testing cycles than is the mere counting of test cases executed, testers running these tests, or the number of hours they spend testing. Such metrics may help measure the quantity of testing, but not the quality of testing. In order to determine the validity of the contractor's assertion, the quality of the testing must be evaluated, and code coverage metrics are the correct method for doing so.

References

1. Beizer, B., *Software Testing Techniques*, Van Nostrand Reinhold, 1990.

2. Jorgensen, P.C., *Software Testing: A Craftsman's Approach*, CRC Press, 2002.

To reduce defects, a project team decided to implement peer reviews for all of their software work products. After about six months into a two-year project it has become evident that the project will take about 2.5 years to complete. Knowing that peer reviews are taking about five percent of the project's effort, the project manager concludes that, to reduce the schedule length, peer reviews would have to be eliminated.

Question Which of the following consequences of ending peer reviews is the best argument for continuing the reviews in order to reduce schedule length?

a) The project's cost will therefore also increase because it costs more to produce code with a high defect density.

b) The project's schedule will most likely be longer because finding defects late in the cycle increases rework and cost.

c) The software product will most likely be released to the customer with significantly more defects than if peer reviews were conducted throughout the life of the project.

d) The project will not realize the advantages of cross training that is a benefit of peer reviews.

Answer: b

Explanation

Indeed, all of the provided answers allude to benefits of peer reviews.

When defect density rises, so does the cost of development. As answer (a) suggests, peer reviews can decrease defect density, so eliminating peer reviews would likely result in a development cost increase. However, the question is asking for a justification related to schedule length, not project cost. Although these two factors are often correlated, answer (b) is more correct than (a).

Similarly, peer reviews can help reduce the number of residual defects contained in the initial release of a system. So, answer (c) does address a very real benefit of peer reviews (fewer errors in the final product), but this benefit is not linked as closely to the development schedule as answer (b).

Development teams can become more effective after experiencing the natural cross-training that occurs during peer reviews. Moreover, the inevitable increased communication and project knowledge among team members can affect the project schedule positively. Yet the cross-training argument supporting peer reviews, particularly as a way to reduce schedule length, is not as strong as the argument presented in answer (b), which highlights the time-intensive rework required after defects are eventually discovered.

In truth, all of these arguments work synergistically toward a reduced schedule length, which is why peer reviews are such a practical and beneficial technique. Studies have shown that peer reviews are one of the most effective ways to detect and correct project defects, and that time spent doing them is a worthwhile investment. It would be counterproductive to eliminate peer reviews as a means to "save time." Nonetheless, if a single argument has to be chosen, answer (b) most directly addresses the relationship between schedule length and peer reviews.

References

1. Futrell, R.T., Shafer, D.F., and Shafer, L.I., *Quality Software Project Management*, Prentice-Hall, 2002.

2. McConnell, S., *Software Project Survival Guide*, Microsoft Press, 1998.

3. Weigers, K.E., *Peer Reviews in Software*, Addison-Wesley, 2002.

4. Wilson, R.C., *Software Rx*, Prentice-Hall, 1997.

An organization has instituted a policy that mandates that postproject reviews be conducted for all software releases. Unhappy with this new policy, Jo Project Manager requests to senior management that it be rescinded. Jo argues that on average about half of her development team is spending too much time going to postproject review meetings for each software release. These meetings are adding a significant amount of effort to the project schedule and budget. At those meetings, the team is often asked to take on additional tasks, and the project manager has instructed them to push back and not take on any additional tasks. In addition to the postproject review meetings, a significant amount of time is spent summarizing the required project data. The bottom line is that the project manager sees no benefit to spending the effort to conducting a postproject review.

Question What should senior management do?

a) Conduct an analysis of the postproject review process to determine the return on investment, with the aim of improving the process.

b) Rescind the policy requiring postproject reviews.

c) Hold the project manger accountable for using the data gathered through the postproject review process to set clear and achievable goals for future projects.

d) Request that the project manager conduct a return on investment analysis for the current postproject review process to demonstrate that the postproject reviews are a waste of time.

Answer: a

Explanation

By no means should the manager rescind the policy. The process may need to be optimized, but the reviews should not be eliminated, lest the benefits of postproject reviews be lost entirely.

The return on investment analysis idea has merit, and such an analysis may change the way the reviews are conducted. However, the project manager is already demonstrably agitated by the review process, so Jo Project Manager would not be a good choice to conduct the analysis. It would be better for a more impartial party to conduct the study.

The project manager should indeed be held accountable for findings from the postproject reviews, insofar as such findings are within the scope of the manager's control. However, answer (c) does not address the manager's concerns about the review process, which appears to be cumbersome.

As answer (a) mentions, an analysis of the postproject review process is warranted, because the process may need improvement. The best course of action is not to eliminate the process [as answer (b) suggests], nor stubbornly adhere to the current process [as answer (c) suggests], but to review and optimize the process [as answer (a) suggests].

References

1. Glass, R.L., *Facts and Fallacies of Software Engineering*, Addison-Wesley, 2003.

2. McConnell, S., *Software Project Survival Guide*, Microsoft Press, 1998.

You are a requirements engineer working on a project to develop a new racing game for a popular video game system. The game's features are based on the plot of an upcoming movie that your company has licensed the rights to use. The game's delivery date is to coincide with the release of the movie. Your organization has experience in developing educational games, but this genre is new. In order to gain market share in the gaming market, several recent college graduates have been hired as developers.

Question   Which of the following is NOT an argument for utilizing the waterfall model?

a)   The game's functional and nonfunctional requirements are well defined.

b)   The waterfall model mimics software development's problem-solving process.

c)   Subsequent versions of the game are not needed; only one version will be delivered.

d)   Coding can begin after the game's graphics, layout, and features are completely designed.

Answer: b

Explanation

The waterfall model can be an appropriate development paradigm, especially when requirements are completely defined, and a single release of the system is planned. Therefore, answers (a) and (c) are indeed valid arguments for selecting the waterfall model.

The waterfall model depicts development as a step-by-step process, beginning with requirements analysis and proceeding through design, coding, and testing. It implicitly assumes that work in one stage is complete before work in the next stage commences. Although answer (d) agrees with this assumption, answer (b) does not. Except in trivial applications, it is difficult for developers to strictly adhere to the waterfall model's rigid depiction of development; this explains why many of the more incremental and iterative models have become more prominent as systems have grown more complex.

Software development is a cerebral, problem-solving process, not a manufacturing process. As such, developers typically analyze their progress, wrestle with trade-offs, and incorporate improvements as the system's architecture, design, and implementation evolve. Although the waterfall methodology is a vast improvement over an ad-hoc approach, it is somewhat "idealized" in that it does not account for the inevitable forward- and backward-looking analyses typically encountered in a real and complex development effort.

References

1. Pfleeger, S.L., *Software Engineering*, Prentice-Hall, 2001.

2. Topper, A., Ouellette, D., and Jorgensen, P., *Structured Methods*, McGraw-Hill, 1994.

You are a requirements engineer working on a project to develop a new racing game. Your organization has experience in developing educational games, but this genre is new. In order to gain market share in the gaming market, your organization needs to deliver a next-generation product. Several features are planned, which require hardware that is itself under development. You have access to the hardware, which introduces some risk. Thankfully, the development schedule is much longer than that of typical game development projects. In order to maximize user satisfaction, your organization can pay local high school students to play the game while it is in development.

Question The company is reexamining the life cycle development model to be used for this product. Which of the following life cycle models will enable you to leverage user feedback during the development of the game?

     I.   *Waterfall*

    II. *Spiral*

   III. *Evolutionary*

   IV. *Code-and-fix*

a)   III and IV

b)   II and III

c)   I and III

d)   II and IV

Answer: b

Explanation

The code-and-fix methodology provides feedback only in an informal and haphazard manner. It can be eliminated from consideration, particularly in this situation: a company delving into a new domain, using new hardware, and attempting to gain significant market share with a next-generation product.

Relatively limited user feedback occurs within waterfall development; this feedback typically happens in the form of reviews and sign-offs between the major stages of the development. This is not the kind of flexible, frequent, and dynamic process model that would fully utilize the feedback from the high school students.

The spiral model, with its repeated calls for rapid prototypes, would be a legitimate candidate. It would encourage developers to mitigate the risks of using new hardware and developing within a new gaming genre, while allowing the incorporation of ongoing feedback from the high school gamers.

Likewise, evolutionary development, which uses incremental releases coupled with aggressive utilization of feedback on completed portions of the system, would be a legitimate methodology choice. Since this project's complete development cycle is unrushed, developers could gradually develop the system over time, then collect and analyze feedback after each version is completed. This incremental development is a sound approach for developing the game itself, while simultaneously allowing for the gradual adoption of the new hardware.

References

1. Larman, C., *Agile and Iterative Development*, Addison-Wesley, 2004.

2. McConnell, S., *Rapid Development*, Microsoft Press, 1996.

3. Paulish, D.J., *Architecture-Centric Software Project Management*, Addison-Wesley, 2002.

Question Cleanroom software engineering techniques:

a) Emphasize defect prevention rather than defect removal

b) Minimize formal verification practices

c) Do not require a well-defined software development process

d) Require that each member of the development team has a unique responsibility

Answer: a

Explanation

The term 'cleanroom' comes from analogy with the cleanrooms associated with chip fabrication. Rather than trying to clean the chips after they are made, the object is to prevent any foreign material from getting into the fabrication environment. Similarly, with the cleanroom method, the aim is to write the code correctly the first time, rather than trying to identify bugs once they have already been introduced into the code. Cleanroom software engineering techniques require the use of well-defined software engineering processes and the formal verification of errors. The delegation of team roles is flexible; a team member may have two or more defined roles.

Reference

1. Prowell, S. J., et al., *Cleanroom Software Engineering: Technology and Process*, Addison-Wesley, 1999.

Area editor: Susan K. Land

X. Software Engineering Tools and Methods

A)   Management tools and methods
B)   Development tools and methods
C)   Maintenance tools and methods
D)   Support tools and methods

Question Which of the following features is *not* part of a typical software configuration management repository tool set?

a) Versioning
b) Requirements tracing
c) Audit trails
d) Risk projection

Answer: d

Explanation

Risk projection is a planning process that rates risks according to the likelihood that the risk is real and the consequences of the problems associated with the risk, should it occur. Although there are risks associated with configuration management, assessment of those risks is not typically part of a configuration management tool set.

Versioning, requirements tracing, and audit trails are all part of a typical software configuration management repository tool set. Versioning refers to the management of extant multiple versions of a particular work product. Versioning allows for multiple versions of work products to be saved, and for users to roll back to previous versions during testing and debugging.

Requirements tracing is an important feature in software configuration management, as it facilitates consistency among the various work products. Finally, audit trails establish when, why, and by whom various changes are made. Tracking such changes is an important part of software configuration management.

Reference

1. Pressman, R., *Software Engineering: A Practitioner's Approach*, 6th ed., McGraw-Hill, 2004.

2	X A	SOFTWARE ENGINEERING TOOLS AND METHODS

SOFTWARE ENGINEERING TOOLS AND METHODS
Management tools and methods

Question Which of the following would *not* be produced as an output when using a software cost estimation tool?

a) Project effort in person-months
b) Project duration
c) Project size
d) Project cost

Answer: c

Explanation

Project size is a typical *input* to a cost estimation tool. Obviously, the size of the project is an essential factor that must be provided *a priori* in order to estimate cost and effort. It goes without saying that a large project is going to cost more than a smaller project; this information must be provided to the tool.

Effort, duration, and cost are all closely related and are all typical outputs from the cost estimation process. Effort is typically expressed in person-months. Duration is a function of effort and team size, whereas cost is a function of effort and labor rates.

Thus, a typical cost estimation tool will take project size as an input and produce effort as an output. Duration and cost are then derived from effort.

Reference

1. Pressman, R., *Software Engineering: A Practitioner's Approach*, 6th ed., McGraw-Hill, 2004.

Question Which of the following techniques is used to establish operational limits for acceptable process variations?

a) Statistical process control

b) Problem management

c) Zero defects

d) Post production repair and rework

Answer: a

Explanation

Statistical process control (SPC), also called statistical quality control (SQC), integrates quality control into each stage of production. Where the traditional focus of quality is typically quality by inspection, SPC implements the concept of quality by prevention. SPC is a technique that employs statistical tools for controlling and improving processes and is an important contributor to continuous process-improvement strategies.

SPC aims to improve processes through causal analysis, a quality-management approach to software development that uses the data resulting from inspections as a means of achieving quality improvements in associated development processes. The ultimate goal of causal analysis is defect prevention. The clear benefit is higher product quality and improved productivity through reductions in rework. The software inspection process is in itself a prevention technique, but the statistics obtained from this process must be augmented with in-depth study to find out what caused the defects. The goals of causal analysis are:

- To identify problem areas in the development process in a systematic way

- To move toward a common corrective action process in which all developers learn from their collective mistakes

- To improve development processes to prevent repetition of mistakes

SPC differs from other, more traditional approaches — such as problem management, zero defects, and repairing and reworking products after they have been produced — in that it focuses on using the development processes to reduce the causes of defects and to improve the quality of the software.

References

1. Malonis, J., *Encyclopedia of Business*, 2nd ed., Gale Group, 2000.

2. McGarry, John, *Practical Software Measurement: Objective Information for Decision Makers*, Addison-Wesley, 2001.

| 4 | X | Software Engineering Tools and Methods |
| | B | Development tools and methods |

Question Which of the following CASE tools would be more suitable to determine the presence of unreachable code within source code:

a) Programming tool
b) Static code analysis tool
c) Test management tool
d) Reengineering tool

Answer: b

Explanation

A tool supporting computer-aided software engineering (CASE tool) implements a technique for using computers to help with one or more phases of the software life cycle, including the systematic analysis, design, implementation, and maintenance of software.

Tedious tasks are ideal candidates for automation. Code coverage, mathematical calculations, simulations, and human-intensive tasks are virtually impossible to do on any sizable scale without using a tool. Static code analysis tools are CASE tools that can be used to determine cyclomatic complexity and identify unreachable code. Automated test-management tools can be used to control and coordinate software testing for each of the major testing steps. CASE reengineering tools support reverse engineering, code restructuring, and database modifications.

References

1. Craig, R. and Jaskiel, S., *Systematic Software Testing*, Artech House, 2002.

2. S. Pfleeger, *Software Engineering Theory and Practice*, 2nd ed., Prentice-Hall, 1998.

XI. Software Quality

While developing a software product, a development team performs verification of the following:

- Proper sequences of events, inputs, outputs, interfaces, and logic flow
- Allocation of timing and sizing budgets
- Error definition, isolation, and recovery
- Proper treatment of safety, security, and other critical requirements

Question   Which of the following types of activity were they performing?

a)   Design verification
b)   Contract verification
c)   Code verification
d)   Process verification

Answer: a

Explanation

Section 6.4.2.4 of ISO/IEC 12207.0 describes design verification as being defined by the following criteria:

a. The design is correct and consistent with and traceable to requirements.

b. The design implements proper sequence of events, inputs, outputs, interfaces, logic flow, allocation of timing and sizing budgets, and error definition, isolation, and recovery.

c. Selected design can be derived from requirements.

d. The design implements safety, security, and other critical requirements correctly, as shown by suitably rigorous methods.

References

1. *Industry Implementation of International Standard ISO/IEC 12207: 1995 Standard for Information Technology — Software Lifecycle Processes,* IEEE Press, 1996.

Question   An engineer has been tasked to evaluate the peer review process being used to support the development of the company's new software product. The task would be considered

a)   Quality control
b)   Quality assurance
c)   Quality measurement
d)   Quality improvement

Answer: b

Explanation

The IEEE Standard for Software Engineering Terminology defines quality control as (1) "a set of activities designed to evaluate the quality of developed or manufactured products" and (2) "the process of verifying one's own work or that of a co-worker." This standard also defines quality assurance as (1) "a planned and systematic pattern of all actions necessary to provide adequate confidence that an item or product conforms to established technical requirements", and (2) "a set of activities designed to evaluate the process by which products are developed or manufactured."

To summarize, quality assurance is a set of activities designed to evaluate a process by which products are developed, whereas quality control is defined as a set of activities designed to evaluate the quality of a developed product.

Reference

1. *IEEE Standard 610.12, IEEE Standard for Software Engineering Terminology,* IEEE Press, 1990 (R2002).

You are testing a gadget, the "new new thing", for your pre-IPO startup company, New New Thing Inc. You know your competition just released their product, but they have gotten really bad press because of its poor quality. You want to wow your customers and investors with a cool gadget that actually works. From your competitor's experience (you have been following their product release very closely), you know the customer wants an availability of at least 99% and a rate of fault occurrence of less than 2 per 8-hour work period.

After the last fixes to your code, you have been testing your product around the clock for 6 days. The product failed a total of 27 times during this period and it took an average of 32 minutes to restart the product after each failure (mainly because of the difficulty of getting to the very small and poorly placed hardware reset button — it is placed on the back of your very heavy gadget and your gadget is always placed under a desk).

Question What is the availability of your product?

a) 60%
b) 90%
c) 10%
d) 99.6%

Answer: b

Explanation

Product availability can be calculated using the following formula:

- Down time = # failures * average time down
- Down time = 27 * 32 = 864
- Total time = Number of days * hours in day * minutes in hour
- Total time = 6 * 24 * 60 = 8640
- Fraction down = Down time/total time
- Fraction down = 864/8640 = 0.1
- Fraction up = 1 – Fraction down
- Fraction up = 1 – 0.1 = 0.9
- Availability = 90%

Reference

1. Sommerville, I., *Software Engineering*, 6th ed., Addison-Wesley, 2001.

Question Quality assurance may be applied to:

    I.   *Requirements*

    II.   *Design*

    III. *Code*

    IV. *Testing*

a)   I and II only
b)   I, II, and III only
c)   I, II, III, and IV
d)   IV only

Answer: c

Explanation

Section 6.3 of ISO/IEC 12207.0 describes quality assurance as follows:

"The Quality Assurance Process is a process for providing adequate assurance that the software products and processes in the project life cycle conform to their specified requirements and adhere to their established plans.   To be unbiased, quality assurance needs to have organizational freedom and authority from persons directly responsible for developing the software product or executing the process in the project.   Quality assurance may be internal or external depending on whether evidence of product or process quality is demonstrated to the management of the supplier or the acquirer.   Quality assurance may make use of the results of other supporting processes, such as Verification, Validation, Joint Reviews, Audits, and Problem Resolution."

The phrase "software products and processes in the project life cycle conform to their specified requirements and adhere to their established plans" is an inclusive statement identifying that all aspects of the project lifecycle are candidates for the application of quality assurance.

Reference

1. *Industry Implementation of International Standard ISO/IEC 12207: 1995 Standard for Information Technology — Software Lifecycle Processes*, IEEE Press, 1996.

A technical lead is working on an iterative life cycle project that is creating a well-understood application using a technology familiar to the development team. The project has 10 major use cases to implement; two have just been delivered on schedule in the first iteration. At the request of the project manager, who is concerned about the amount of effort being spent fixing defects, the lead has collected some data on quality performance during the first iteration. The data shows that planned reviews of requirements and design are not occurring. It shows that 22 defects are being detected during unit and system testing per 100 SLOC.

Question   The lead thinks the defect rate seems high for the nature of this project. Which of the following would be the most effective approach to develop support for this hypothesis?

a)   Analyzing industry data for this type of project
b)   Asking knowledgeable colleagues working on different projects in the organization
c)   Asking team members with the most quality experience
d)   Analyzing data from previous projects from within the organization

Answer: d

Explanation

It is recommended that data on the numbers of defects be collected. The numbers and types of defects should be among the outputs of the basic quality measures associated with any development effort. Comparing the current project's defect data to that of other similar projects is the best way to determine whether this project is deviating from expected norms. Since this is not a new type of project for the organization, data from previous projects will provide the strongest predictor of expected performance.

References

1. SEI, *Capability Maturity Model Integration (CMMI), Version 1.1,* CMU/SEI-2002-TR-029, Software Engineering Institute, Carnegie Mellon University, 2002.

2. Humphrey, W., *Managing the Software Process,* Addison-Wesley, 1989.

Mary, a technical lead of a software development team, is working on an iterative life cycle project that is creating a well-understood application using a technology familiar to the team. The project has 10 major use cases to implement; two have just been delivered on schedule in the first iteration. At the request of the project manager, who is concerned about the amount of effort being spent fixing defects, Mary has collected some data on quality performance during the first iteration. The data shows that planned reviews of requirements and design are not occurring. It shows that 22 defects are being detected during unit and system testing per 100 SLOC.

Question Mary is asked to devise a solution to reduce the amount of overall effort relating to defects. The highest leverage activity would be to:

a) Perform more testing earlier
b) Review requirements and designs
c) Hold more code reviews
d) Give developers more time to write code

Answer: b

Explanation

Testable requirements are described in the Capability Maturity Model Integration (CMMI) document and in IEEE Std 830, *IEEE Standard for Software Requirements Specifications*. The identification of how a requirement will be tested can prevent the implementation of a bad requirement that would introduce errors at a later point in the development life cycle of the application. As the development life cycle progresses it becomes more and more expensive to fix defects. Defects identified during the requirements and design phases can be more cheaply fixed and more easily corrected.

References

1. *IEEE Std 830-1998, IEEE Standard for Software Requirements Specifications,* IEEE Press, 1998.

2. SEI, *Capability Maturity Model Integration (CMMI), Version 1.1, CMU/SEI-2002-TR-029,* Software Engineering Institute Carnegie Mellon University, 2002.

Mary, a technical lead of a software development team, is working on an iterative life cycle project that is creating a well-understood application using a technology familiar to the team. The project has 10 major use cases to implement; two have just been delivered on schedule in the first iteration. At the request of the project manager, who is concerned about the amount of effort being spent fixing defects, Mary has collected some data on quality performance during the first iteration. The data shows that planned reviews of requirements and design are not occurring. It shows that 22 defects are being detected during unit and system testing per 100 SLOC.

Question Mary is asked to predict the defect trend for the project going forward. It is calculated that with no changes in process the defect rate

a) Will likely drop later in the project as kinks are worked out

b) Will remain the same

c) Will likely increase as the project progresses

d) Cannot be predicted at this point

Answer: c

Explanation

The problem states that the team is working on an iterative, or incremental, project life cycle. This life cycle model requires the development of several partial deliverables. Each deliverable is a subset of the next, with each having incrementally more functionality. With no reviews, a high defect rate, and an iterative life cycle, things will only get worse as new code is written. This project is likely to become mired in the classic build/fix scenario. If no improvement is made to the existing process and reviews continue to be ignored, it can only be expected that existing code will contain undetected defects and that further development will increase the number of defects, both detected and undetected.

Reference

1. McConnell, S., *Code Complete*, Microsoft Press, 2002.

Question Which software metric is equal to the number of predicate nodes in a program's flowgraph + 1?

a) Function points

b) Cyclomatic complexity

c) Coupling factor

d) Program volume

Answer: b

Explanation

Cyclomatic complexity is a measure of the logical complexity of a program. It can be viewed as a measure of the number of independent paths in a program's flow graph. There are several equivalent ways to measure cyclomatic complexity:

- Number of regions in the program's flowgraph
- $E - N + 2$, where E is the number of flowgraph edges and N is the number of flowgraph nodes
- Number of predicate flowgraph nodes + 1

Thus, a program with N predicate conditions would have a cyclomatic complexity of N + 1.

Function points are also related to software complexity. Unlike cyclomatic complexity, which is based on source code, function points constitute a source-code-independent metric. Function points are applied to the specification of a software system, and are based on counting elements such as number of external inputs, external outputs, external inquiries, internal logical files, and external interface files.

Coupling factor is an OO design metric from the MOOD metrics suite for measuring coupling between classes. In general, coupling is a measure of the degree to which one module depends on another. The more one module depends on another, the higher the overall complexity. On the other hand, programs with greater independence among modules tend to be lower in complexity. Coupling factor is a formalization of this general notion of coupling for object-oriented software, and is not related to the number of program predicates.

Program volume is a measure of complexity from an approach developed by Halstead in the 1970's called software science. It is based on the number of distinct operators and operands that occur in the program. Like coupling factor, it is also not related to the number of predicates occurring in the program.

Reference

1. Pressman, R., *Software Engineering: A Practitioner's Approach*, 6th ed., McGraw-Hill, 2004.

9	XI	SOFTWARE QUALITY	
	A		Software quality concepts

Question Which of the following are among the main purposes of software inspections?

I.   *Check whether standards have been followed*

II.   *Determine product suitability for its intended use*

III. *Detect defects*

IV.   *Become familiar with the product*

a) II and IV only.
b) III and IV only.
c) IV only.
d) I and III only.

Answer: d

Explanation

IEEE standard 1012-1998, IEEE Standard for Software Verification and Validation, describes Inspection as follows:

"Inspection: Inspect the software process to detect defects in the product at each selected development stage to assure the quality of the emerging software."

IEEE Standard 610.12, IEEE Standard Glossary of Software Engineering Terminology defines Inspections as follows:

"Inspection: A static analysis technique that relies on visual examination of development products to detect errors, violations of development standards, and other problems."

It follows from these definitions that inspections are used both to detect defects and to determine conformance with applicable standards or processes. They are not used to acquire familiarity with a product or to determine a product's suitability for its intended use.

References

1. IEEE Std 1012-1998, *IEEE Standard for Software Verification and Validation*, IEEE Press, 1998.

2. IEEE Std 610.12-1990 (R2002), *IEEE Standard Glossary of Software Engineering Terminology*, IEEE Press, 1990.

Question Which of the following is NOT applicable to software quality assurance?

a) Pareto's 80/20 Rule
b) Kirchhoff's Law
c) Root cause analysis
d) Failure analysis

Answer: b

Explanation

Items (a), (c), and (d) are applicable to software quality assurance. Pareto's 80/20 rule states "eighty percent of your troubles will come from 20 per cent of your problems". This rule serves as a reminder of the importance of concentrating on problem discovery and resolution. Root cause analysis serves to identify and manage project risk. If the sources of risk can be controlled, they may be preventable. Failure analysis is the systematic examination of failure so that the root cause may be determined. This information may then be used to improve the developed product. All three of these items — Pareto's Rule, root cause analysis, and failure analysis — may be used very appropriately in support of software quality assurance activities.

Kirchhoff's two laws can be described as follows:

> Kirchhoff's Current Law: The current flowing into a node is the same as the current flowing out of that node.

> Kirchhoff's Voltage Law: The sum of all voltage drops around a closed circuit is zero.

These laws are used to analyze series and parallel circuits. They are clearly not relevant to software quality assurance.

References

1. Pressman, R. S., *Software Engineering: A Practitioner's Approach,* 6th ed., McGraw-Hill, 2005.

2. Alexander, C. and Sadiku, M. N. O., *Fundamentals of Electric Circuits*, 2nd ed., McGraw-Hill, 2004.

Question   During the inspection of the code for the emergency braking system of a new high-speed train (a highly critical, real-time application), the review team identifies several characteristics of the code. Which of these characteristics are generally viewed as UNDESIRABLE?

    I.   *The code contains three recursive functions.*

    II. *The computation of acceleration uses floating-point arithmetic.*

    III. *All other computations use integer arithmetic.*

    IV. *The code contains one linked list that uses dynamic memory allocation.*

    V. *All inputs are checked to determine that they are within expected bounds before they are used.*

a)   I and IV only
b)   III and V only
c)   I, II, and IV only
d)   I, II, III, and IV only

Answer: c

Explanation

The answer is (c) because recursion, floating-point, and linked lists with dynamic memory allocation are all undesirable in safety critical programming. Recursion is problematic because recursive functions can in general not be guaranteed to terminate, have unpredictable execution time, and have unknown memory requirements. The use of floating point arithmetic cannot guarantee accuracy of computations, so it should not be used in safety-critical applications. Linked lists are to be avoided because they may cause memory overflow problems and may fail unpredictably because of memory allocation problems.

References

1. Marcus, E. and Stern, H., *Blueprints for High Availability*, 2nd ed., John Wiley and Sons, 2003.

A new organization is working on its first product, an online service to enable instructional videos to be viewed on demand. The company also intends to partner with other companies so that prospective customers can also buy the materials needed to produce an instructional video. The product is currently in the testing phase.

Question Under time pressure, a testing team has been testing the code produced by a programming team. A member of the testing team drafted bug reports for some issues that need attention, and has informed the author of the code. After two hours, the programmer e-mails the tester and says that those bugs have been fixed. Which of the following is the BEST course of action to ensure that the product is of the highest quality?

a) Since the issues are resolved, you can move on to the next testing tasks for the system.

b) Promptly conduct follow-up tests to make sure that the issues are fixed.

c) Promptly conduct follow-up tests with different data than the initial test to ensure that the issue is really fixed.

d) Conduct regression tests on the code overnight in order to save time. The tester's time is better served detecting new issues.

Answer: c

Explanation

How a tester follows up a programmer's rework impacts the quality of the product. Answer (a) would not be an appropriate response, because the tester should not just take the programmer's word, even if time is critical.

Answer (b) is getting closer to the recommended solution. Although testing the updated code is important, the problem may have been fixed enough to satisfy the original test case but the issue may not be completely resolved. Answer (d) is overkill, since the testing process should not stop for one issue. Each issue should be promptly and thoroughly examined so that it can be resolved and testing can continue.

The correct answer, answer (c), requires the prompt testing of the problem. Using different data allows confirmation that the issue has been truly resolved.

Reference

1. Kaner, C., Back, J., and Pettichord, B., *Lessons Learned in Software Testing*, John Wiley & Sons, 2002.

Printed in the United States
216705BV00003B/1/P